(a guide to relishing the solo life)

living alone & loving it

barbara feldon

A Fireside Book
Published by Simon & Schuster
New York   London   Toronto   Sydney

FIRESIDE
Rockefeller Center
1230 Avenue of the Americas
New York, NY 10020

For information about special discounts for bulk purchases,
please contact Simon & Schuster Special Sales:
1-800-456-6798 or business@simonandschuster.com
Designed by William Ruoto
Manufactured in the United States of America
7 9 10 8 6

Library of Congress Cataloging-in-Publication Data
Feldon, Barbara.
Living alone & loving it : a guide to relishing the solo life /
Barbara Feldon.
p. cm.
"A Fireside book."
1. Single people—Life skills guides. 2. Living alone. I. Title: Living
alone and loving it. II. Title.
HQ800 .F24 2003
646.7'0086'52—dc21   2002026789

ISBN-13: 978-0-7432-3517-4
ISBN-10:   0-7432-3517-7

for Leo Stone

acknowledgments

I'm grateful to many people whose support and input have graced these pages: my beloved sister, Pat Koleser, for being my North Star; Buddy Mantia for his enthusiasm and anchoring friendship; and Molly Peacock, my cheerleader, inspiration and surrogate sister.

I'm thankful for the exquisite gifts of my agent, Kathleen Anderson, whose attention to every phase of this book has been invaluable, and I'm enormously indebted to the keen eye and enriching midwifery of my Simon & Schuster editor, Doris Cooper. If I flagged along the way, David Schulman coaxed me forward on Friday nights when we shared our projects and Thai food.

I'm also indebted to so many men and women who shared their living-alone perspectives: the lovely contributions of my friend Jan Meshkoff; Ralph Rosenberg, who contributed so much to my life; the inspired living-aloner Diane Morrison; Doris Burkett, who has a huge heart; Bob Stewart, a reliable source of energy and joy; Nan Winton; the intrepid Meg Peterson; Jean Block, my first living-alone mentor; the fervent traveler Lori Misura; Luba Snable; the tap dancing Posi Tucker; Dory Previn for her wisdom; Casey Kelly, who created our goal group; my dear friend Burt Nodella, who is the CEO of living alone; and many others who have allowed me to harvest their experiences.

I am fortunate to have in my heart endearing memories of Jan Stussy, a magician of life, and Leo Stone, who offered me the gift of owning myself.

contents

prologue

When I was a kid the greatest thrill I experienced at the circus was watching the flying trapeze artists. High in the pastel lights at the top of the tent, a young woman in sparkling tights swooped through space secure in the grip of her partner. Suddenly, he would let go and send her flying above the gasping crowd. Then, just as she'd begin to fall, another partner would swing down to snatch her up. I imagined that I was her in thrilling flight, tossed from one pair of masculine hands to another.

It felt sublime.

Years later, I realized how ardently I'd always hoped to find salvation in the arms of a man; a deep, intimate, soul-satisfying union with a strong partner who would cherish, comfort and in many ways support me. For a while fate bowed to my wishes, but when it finally balked and I found myself alone, I felt as if I were falling through space. There were no outstretched arms in sight and I hadn't rigged a safety net.

ↄ

As a child I absorbed the idea that all true happiness was mated happiness. Period. Every grown-up I knew was married. In our suburban Pittsburgh neighborhood there was a daily choreography of fathers leaving in the morning and mothers, at twilight, bathing, dressing, powdering and combing in preparation for their husband's return, a dance that echoed my grandparents' routine. When my dad appeared each evening he stood near my mother as she cooked in the steamy kitchen and shared the news of his day at the office; they sipped scotch on the rocks and, in my eyes, looked as glamorous as Myrna Loy and William Powell. I gazed from the doorway, dreamy with desire to grow up and play Mother's role in my own intimate drama.

As I progressed from envious onlooker at older girls' weddings to bridesmaid—launching friends through the wedding march to star in white tulle at the altar— I welcomed the inevitability of a coupled future and its foreverness. Although I entertained embryonic notions of an unconventional (whatever that meant) life as an actress, my imaginings never consciously perched on the idea of living my life without a mate.

Immediately after graduating drama school I raced to New York City where I lucked into the most conventional of unconventional apartments, a sixth-floor walk-up, cold-water flat in Greenwich Village complete with regiments of cockroaches. It was perfect! When the picture was further embellished by meeting and falling in love with a Belgian who looked like a movie star, spoke with a French accent and ordered arcane wines, I knew I was finally starring on the silver screen of my life.

I regretted giving up my Village pad—my first taste of independence—but family pressure and my ardor for Lucien overcame my resistance and I prepared to marry. Then, minutes before the ceremony, I was attacked by a sniper of ambivalence and balked at the vow to "obey." I sprinted to the minister's study to plead that he remove it from the ceremony, but he refused and laughed off my distress with, "Oh, just say it and don't mean it." Unsatisfied, I stood at the altar where I had dreamed of standing, where my mother and grandmother had stood. But instead of feeling joy over a sacred bonding, tears ran down my face at having sworn to a vow (and the servitude it implied) I couldn't tolerate, a vow that Mother and Grandmother had repeated without flinching. To me it hinted that my life was no longer my own.

My reaction was a symptom, an early, tiny crack in the veneer of mated roles. I had pictured marriage as a mosaic of bits of colored glass in a kaleidoscope—but turn the kaleidoscope slightly and the shards of glass fall into chaos before forming a new pattern. I felt my life was about to change, and a different kind of life—"for better or for worse"—would bring more role challenges than I had imagined in my mating dream.

My marriage slowly slid from fantasy to chastening reality, but the breakup was made smoother by an uptick in my career and a necessary move to Los Angeles to play Secret Agent "99" in the 1960s television series *Get Smart*. I soon fell in love with my colleague Burt Nodella, with whom I lived for the next twelve years. While our relationship as a couple eventually reached an impasse, we continued to be the dear friends that we are today.

I quickly fell in love again (there was a pattern here) but was startled when, for the first time in my romantic history, I was anticipating a permanent relationship while my partner was veering away from commitment.

A number of my single friends were experiencing parallel adventures. Often partners approached relationships so burdened with bruises from childhood, former love disasters and unrealistic expectations that the romance was overwhelmed. Some simply chose to delay commitment to concentrate on a career; others were exploring the option of living single. For me, now that living alone had become a reality, I experienced it as a negative, a lonely but temporary vacuum between partners; I couldn't imagine it becoming a chronic condition. As the years passed I was forced to view it differently. There's an old saying: "Wisdom is accepting the obvious."

The "obvious" includes the soaring divorce rate. Now there are a startling number of people living alone— nearly twenty-six million projected nationwide—and according to the 2000 census, the number of people living alone is now greater than the number of nuclear families. A husky 48 percent of Manhattanites live alone. We've become a mighty horde! Whether we are casualties of emotional wars, single due to the death of a companion or unpartnered by choice, for the first time in history, living alone is an established way of life.

&

I first conceived of writing this book in 1977 as a sort of therapeutic exercise. I was newly alone and scared, and my self-esteem was flagging. Wasn't a woman without a man somehow flawed? Would I ever be with someone again? Was I doomed to endure a second-rate life? I was embarrassed by the barely submerged pity in the question, "Have you met anyone yet?" as though my love life was my only life. But as I gradually ceased judging myself by my romantic status and began to harvest the pleasures of friends and creative interests, the grisly future I had imagined morphed into an enjoyable present. I began to relish my single status and set the book aside.

But over the years I've become aware of the great numbers of singles who consider living alone a holding pen until their "significant" lives with a validating mate begin. Some suffer from societal pressure to marry, or from the sense that they are missing out on the "ideal" of married bliss, and many of them experience acute loneliness and longing.

But living alone doesn't mean you *are* alone. Singles are members of an enormous and vital segment of society.

Living on one's own is not always ideal—but then, nei-ther is marriage. The mated format is charted territory. Those venturing into singlehood are the Lewis and Clarks of a pioneering lifestyle with few maps, unex-pected ambushes and an infinity of adventures. Therein lies its glory!

I admit I'm writing from a bias. I was in two com-mitted relationships over a period of many years and I'm grateful for the experience. But I've lived alone now for more than two decades, for which I am equally thankful.

Living alone deserves our praise.

It is an opportunity to take the raw material of time and sculpt it like Play-Doh. We can bask in a pool of soli-tude or invite the world to join us. We can create, travel, learn (living-aloners could be an intellectual elite!) and change directions as playfully as sea otters; we can dis-cover who we are and freely strive toward whom we might become.

Our happiness is in our own hands.

Like a colt on new legs we're encouraged to practice autonomy and free ourselves from crippling dependency.

But most beautifully, living alone is an invitation to freely connect with others. Though I'd be a fool to say that there is anything sweeter than devoted companionship at its best, living alone wins hands down in terms of personal blossoming and rewarding friendships.

The issue isn't living alone—it's living fully.

I'm not advocating any particular model, but by sharing my experiences and those of friends who enjoy living on their own, I hope to encourage other singles to tailor their lives in ways unique to them. My purpose is not to demonstrate how to "make do" until Mr. or Ms. Right comes along, but to shake off the stigma of the lonely spinster or eccentric bachelor and accept living alone as a lifestyle offering fulfillment equal to (though different from) that of being mated. For 50 percent of Americans marriage is forever; for the rest of us there is another adventure.

There is more than one way to feel complete.

In a Buddhist story a Zen master hangs his disciple out over an abyss clinging to a slender branch—and asks him to let go. If the disciple has the courage, he will do so, then fall into the abyss, "land on his own feet and never poach on another's land." Living alone is not what I would have chosen. But when it chose me, I ceased clinging to the branch of expectations and dependencies (which I did most unwillingly) and risked the dreaded fall. I landed on my feet and realized that this new geography was a gift. Only here could I commandeer my own life and experience the adventures and, yes, the raptures of living on my own.

The French poet Apollinaire captured the moment magnificently:

> *"Come to the edge."*
> *"It's too high."*
> *"Come to the edge."*
> *"We might fall."*
> *"Come to the edge."*
> *And they came*
> *And he pushed them*
> *And they flew!*

What comes is not to be avoided
what goes is not to be followed.
—MASTER DAIBAI

living alone

(freedom is hard to love)

It is Saturday morning in Manhattan. I wake up today in my wallpapered room tucked over my neighbors' courtyard gardens. The spring foliage is transparent in the sun, birds chirp from the comfort of branches; all else is silent. After living alone for twenty years I'm still filled with arias of praise for the blessings of my sweet solitude.

But I haven't always felt this way.

We complex creatures have a baffling talent for entertaining two opposite desires at the same time. Even while I was intoxicated by the idea of merging with an imagined beloved, I got a renegade thrill from contemplating living independently, freely choosing pleasures to include and intrusions to exclude in order to allow my life to sing. "Owning myself" had the allure of an exotic perfume.

As a child I would lie in bed at night listening to my parents' sleep-burdened breathing and dare myself to creep downstairs, sneak out the locked front door and sample the thrill of simply standing under the stars by myself. The anarchy of such freedom was spiritual ambrosia to a girl who rankled under the restrictions of childhood. But I wasn't yet brave enough to risk it.

On our property, hidden from the view of the main house, was an old pony shed—alas, without a pony— with a slanted, scratchy roof onto which I would climb on summer afternoons. By escaping to my miniature sanctuary I was expressing a need for independence— difficult to experience in the buzz of family life—while at the same time feeling reassured that my parents were within calling distance. I continued my ambivalence about solitude through college; though I envied girls with private rooms, I was relieved by having the company of roommates.

Then, after graduation, just as I was about to launch

into the world on my own, I fell in love with and married Lucien.

Although for many years I embraced bonded companionship enthusiastically, always there was that lingering desire to live by myself. After our marriage ended and during my second relationship, with Burt, I once playfully floated the idea to him of our living next door to each other. I was charmed by the prospect of a personal space to which I could retreat at will in unaccompanied splendor. When he laughed off my fantasy I didn't persist, there being no precedent for such a maverick arrangement. Nevertheless, I continued to be fascinated by the lifestyles of the single women I met. Carla, a costume designer, lived by herself in the Hollywood Hills in a cottage decorated with Moroccan tiles that she had gathered on one of her adventures abroad. She traveled alone but she rarely ended up that way, often meeting people who invited her into their homes or, upon occasion, into their beds. And, though Burt and I lamented Carla's unwillingness to settle into a traditional relationship, I was aware that she seemed to have thrived on her choices.

As time went on and our relationship deteriorated, we were forced to realize that having no relationship might be better than having an unworkable one and I took comfort in the prospect of exploring another way of living. On Saturdays, while Burt was sailing, I looked around for a studio apartment that I imagined decorating capriciously, a hideaway like a secret garden to which there is only one key. I even began to collect things: dessert dishes with strawberries painted on them, a fluffy comforter; objects I bought and simply left in the stores to be retrieved only in my solo future.

But when the break actually came and we were separated not only formally but by an entire continent, the freedom that I had happily envisioned turned sinister and ambushed me at night. I dreamed that I was in a damp prison cell when suddenly the doors swung open and I was free. After walking confidently through an icy, barren landscape, I stopped, turned and resolutely walked right back into prison.

Freedom is hard to love, I discovered.

Bereft of the security of my relationship and without another one waiting in the wings, I felt like an astronaut whose umbilical tie to the spaceship had been severed and was doomed to drift alone through an endless universe. I was tethered to no one—and perhaps never again would be.

Not long after our breakup I arrived in London for a television performance, and the city cooperated soggily with my baleful mood. One dank afternoon I was in a taxi on my way to an appointment and I decided to get out and walk. I intended to say to the driver, "You can let me out here, I'm early." But instead I blurted out, "You can let me out here, I'm lonely!" I was woefully in need of direction, preferably in the form of a role model, someone who had climbed the mountain of aloneness and was perched there comfortably. Could such a person exist? Could anyone endure, with equanimity, what I was suffering through?

I called my publicist and told her a lie, that I was going to write an article for an American magazine on women who lived alone successfully. Did she know anyone? Surprisingly, she did.

A week later I sat across from Pam in a cozy English tearoom sipping Darjeeling and munching on scones smeared with clotted cream. She seemed puzzled by some of my, as the English say, "queries." Yes, she regarded living alone as a splendid way of life; she needed lots of solitude in order to write her novel.

"Do you eat dinner alone?" I queried.

"Oh, no, not usually. Since I'm by myself writing all day, it's rather nice, isn't it, to have a meal with a friend."

I was alert to her jaunty practicality.

"Do you travel by yourself?" (To test my courage I'd been planning extended trips alone to places where no English was spoken.)

"I have done that, and it's OK, but I find it's actually more fun to travel with friends."

Pam was divorced and had no man in her life, but it didn't concern her a bit. "Is she for real?" I wondered.

"Don't you miss living with a man?" I asked.

"Oh heavens, no!" she laughed. "It's so deeply ingrained in me to wait on them that I tend to slip into servitude. Besides," she added merrily, "I've lived so many years without a man it's hard to even imagine doing it again."

"What about . . . intimacy?" I offered wistfully.

"Oh, that's perhaps too personal to go into, except to say that it is, of course, important," she leaned forward, "*very* important."

Before I could pursue this interesting news, Pam looked at me closely and said, "You're rather up against it aren't you."

My cover was blown. I admitted everything: my single status, my unpreparedness, my anxiety, my misery. She was sympathetic but frankly bemused that I regarded the autonomy as a deficit.

Pam became my first mentor and her view of living alone was liberating: *Although I would love to have the pleasure of a companion, if he didn't come along there just might be another way to find fulfillment.*

I wanted to kiss her!

Future mentors would show me how to live alone not just comfortably but joyously. Still, I could not even approach that heady state until I confronted loneliness, the most fearsome dragon of all. Not the garden variety that we all encounter from time to time, but that desolate, hopeless "I'm alone forever" one.

Perhaps all the dragons of our lives are princesses
who are only waiting to see us act, just once,
with beauty and courage.
—RAINER MARIA RILKE

slaying the dragon: loneliness

(we believe there is something essential we
don't have that's obtainable. what we long
for doesn't exist, not anywhere.
the ache is in the belief)

Human connection is everything. It's the whole story, the
meaning of our lives. Living without it we wither. No
wonder the most cruel punishment is solitary confine-
ment. The specter of being isolated has kept many men

and women awake at night and many others glued to unhappy—even lonely—marriages.

As a little girl I lived in dread of solitude, those motherless hours stretching into an eternal Sahara. When Mother, who worked as a bookkeeper for a mayonnaise company, would disappear—with her powdery fragrance and the throaty consolation of her voice—down the steep wooden staircase to the street below, my world would falter and grow dim as those smog-laden mornings of Pittsburgh. My father, a businessman, traveled; my sister was at school and my indifferent caretaker was preoccupied. Only Mother, returning at dusk, could repair my distress.

Beyond being with my mom, my happiest memories were of spending summers with my grandparents, who lived in a white clapboard house on a shady street in Flint, Michigan. Granddad would rise at 4 A.M. to go to the automobile factory. For Grandma, Monday was wash day, Tuesday was ironing. In the summer there was canning to be done, and always there were roomers upstairs who needed tending.

Some evenings Aunt Rene would stop by and we'd all sit on the porch chatting and swinging on the squeaky glider while Granddad would water the balding lawn from the front steps. On sweltering nights he would take my sister and me by the hand and walk us up to Saginaw Boulevard to buy ice-cream cones for the whole family. We'd stroll back in the dark heat with ice cream dripping on our shoes, and our hearts were happy.

No static photo can describe the depth of happiness sitting with my granddad on a hillside under the spangling sky at the Michigan State Fair, my small hand engulfed in his. On weekends we'd pile into his old Ford and rumble off to Uncle Henry's cottage at a lake near Howell where we'd swim out past the squishy mud in sun-warmed water or row around in a lumbering boat with heavy oars. In the cabin, Aunt Louise (who had a thrilling scar across her neck from a goiter operation) would make apple pies.

❧

Those summers with my Michigan relatives that felt so right and safe planted expectations in my mind of what human connectedness could and should be in the future. Later, when I traveled to Italy and Greece, those memories would surface nostalgically when I would watch the easy familiarity among villagers as they promenaded in the town square. As if held in a benevolent palm, grand-mothers, mothers, fathers, children and lovers were tak-ing the dear luxury of company for granted. But here in the United States the secure embrace of families was sadly slipping away.

After leaving home I basked in the reassurance of roommates, boyfriends and marriage. But after I left my second relationship and was—for the first time in my life—without emotional support, the image of myself as a bereft five-year-old erupted unexpectedly like a lurking demon rattling predictions of a desolate life. I reached out to a friend to whom I sheepishly recalled giving sage advice when she was suffering from loneliness after a divorce. At the time, I was still tucked securely in a rela-tionship and smiled indulgently at her fears, bemused by her paralysis in view of the options her freedom pre-sented. Now I was experiencing a humbling appreciation of her pain. I phoned her to commiserate, but when she said she was thriving in a new relationship, I was too embarrassed to admit that our situations had reversed. I hung up feeling deserted and unable to remember the advice I had so breezily offered. I was alone. Irrevocably, miserably, desperately alone. I sank into a hollow morass of abandonment that had been waiting since childhood for an opportunity to swamp me and I felt ashamed that I, an evolved adult, could feel such bleakness.

So I precipitously fled back to Manhattan from Los Angeles after a twelve-year absence. But the salvation I imagined in old friends was illusory. Our lives had changed, we had changed: We no longer shared common interests, some had moved away, some were preoccupied with careers. They were cordial but I was seeking a more potent remedy.

Feeling like a wimp, I was determined to master aloneness and tried the kamikaze approach. I rigorously banned the anesthetic of radio or television and tried to banish people from my mind for days at a time. I deliberately cultivated aloneness, distilled it and, like a hiker taking snake venom to innoculate against rattler bites, created a serum of isolation to boost my abandonment immunity. In this personal deprivation chamber I attempted to wrestle with aloneness, get it in a neck lock and force it to the ground. If Thoreau could do it so could I!

Well, I couldn't. At least not that way. (And who knows how much solitude Thoreau really endured. Even our national hero of "going it alone" apparently managed to leave Walden Pond almost daily to have dinner with his mother or Emerson.) I remembered that as a child I couldn't bear to listen to the sometimes desolate country music that wafted through the radio from nearby West Virginia. One lyric about a cowboy lost on the desert lamented: "All day I pace the barren waste without a trace of water . . ." Now I was pacing that barren waste without an oasis in sight.

❧

A trickle of relief came while having lunch with Leo, an older and very wise friend. When I confessed my loneliness he cheerfully suggested avenues for human warmth that I may have overlooked. For example, why didn't I recognize the dry cleaner or the grocer as fellow travelers who might populate the barren waste?

"Because there's something missing," I explained. "They're strangers, there's no depth to the encounter. When you're with a loved one you feel held in life, secure, safe. The way I felt with my mother and grandfather when I was a child."

"But you're not a child and don't have a child's needs," he said without a trace of admonition. "A child is in danger without company because it's helpless, but an adult has access to any need imaginable: food, medicine, com-

panionship. All an adult has to do is to pick up the phone and call a doctor or drive to the supermarket or meet a friend for coffee."

I was startled by his remark and digested it for a moment before resisting further, "Even so, casual encounters with people can't give me that 'essential' connection that an intimate relationship can."

"Why not?"

That stopped me. For the first time I realized that I'd never considered giving people-in-passing that much importance. In my obsession with intimacy I hadn't paid much attention to the rest of the world.

"You're assigning all the magic you require in relationships to one or two people. What's to stop you from finding it among as many souls as you encounter? Or, better yet," he smiled, "giving up the idea of magic altogether (a jolting prospect!) and simply viewing the world as being full of any number of special people with whom you can connect—*in a variety of ways.*"

"But what about this ache?" I placed my hand dramatically over my heart. "This longing that can only be relieved by a deep involvement?"

He looked at me sympathetically. *"You believe,"* he said gently, *"there's something essential you don't have that's actually obtainable. What you long for doesn't exist, not any-where. The ache is in the belief."*

I realized I was looking for the perfect fix in one ide-alized person.

Then he asked if I'd heard the Zen story told by D. T. Suzuki about the man who is dying of thirst while standing in the middle of a river.

ℯ⌢

Gradually, and I mean very gradually, I began to focus on people I met during the day and tried to believe that they counted as meaningful connections. Because of the rushing crowds in Manhattan there is a tendency to shut down on the street or subway, to retreat inwardly and avoid the incursion of strangers. But each four square blocks of the city is a village stocked with neighborhood familiars and I was chagrined to realize how many peo-ple I saw nearly every day—doormen, delivery people, mailmen, people walking their dogs—with whom I'd never spoken, a large enough river of people to quench anyone's thirst for connection. I began to practice mak-ing eye contact. Many passersby didn't return my gaze, some looked through me, but there were others who frankly acknowledged me with a nod or a smile, and, from time to time, there was an instantaneous connection so joyous that my spirit was lifted for hours. I was surprised at how warming even the briefest encounters could be.

❧

Mary Burton is the manager of the bank on my corner. For months I'd observed her patiently attending to customers, sometimes cajoling them, her ribbon of laughter soaring above the din and bustle of the bank. When an employee's thumb was cut off by the vault door it was Mary who took the woman—and her thumb—to the emergency room, and it was she who aided another employee when he had a stroke, then visited him every day at the hospital and later at his home. At three o'clock she often stood, keys in hand, chatting with a patron before locking the bank door.

One day, after concluding a bank transaction, I asked if she would let me take her to lunch at the cafe in the Whitney Museum. Over cappuccino I listened as she unfolded her childhood story—of virtually raising herself alone—that was as poignant as a novel. I also heard an electrifying account of the bank robbery during which she crouched under her desk whispering to the 911 dispatcher. As I listened to her, really *listened,* I heard something beyond her words; I was hearing Mary herself, her very *being*—with all its colors and layers and textures—resonating through her stories. I realized that when I surrendered myself to a pure state of listening—of *receiving* her—it was impossible to feel lonely.

Mrs. Scully, an older woman whom I'd watched lugging pails of water to nourish the foliage on the street, told me excitedly about each tree, including a diagnosis of the disease devouring our molting ginkgo. I often saw her eating dinner alone in a booth of a nearby coffee shop that I frequented, and I began stopping by her table to chat.

Our seemingly surface conversations about the trees or our block association were openings through which her hunger for simple human connection—something I shared—could be satisfied. When weeks went by without seeing her, I inquired at her building and was saddened to learn that she had suddenly died. The neighborhood—and I—have felt emptier without her.

Encounters with these women were not profoundly intimate *but they contained a sweet ember of humanity that was comforting*. There's a Sufi story of a man who says,

"Master, I've discovered the answer! Knock and the door will be opened to you." The master replied, "Who said the door was closed?" Human warmth had been available all along, I had simply ignored the open door. Thanks to Leo I was beginning to *notice the variety of human connection available instead of obsessing about what is missing.*

❧

Then there was the issue of friends. I'd grown passive during my coupled years. My partner was the oak tree of my social world and everyone else was lesser foliage. Since friendships have a way of blossoming if you shine on them and withering if you don't, I was facing a languishing garden that was badly in need of tending. Ironically, now when I had the most need for people, I had the least skills and inner strength at my command to remedy it.

I began by thinking about connections I'd neglected to value. Guiltily, I made a list of friends whom I'd let drift to the suburbs of my life. True, they'd let me float out of their lives too, but they were more involved with family and had less at stake than I. Reeling in friends who had drifted away was a ragged campaign. They were welcoming but had busy lives, and it would take time for them to get used to including me. I still found myself with uncomfortable patches of time alone.

The most awful days during those early months were holidays when most people I knew had family activities. I hadn't yet learned to *plan ahead for those emotionally laden holidays like Thanksgiving and Christmas.* I would wake to the dreadful thunder of silence in my neighborhood and enviously imagine the world romping at a celebration that excluded me.

But even as I was flirting with self-pity, there was, right under my nose, a folder crammed with unanswered letters dating back, I'm mortified to admit, seven years. People *had* reached out to me and, though I sincerely cared for them, I'd allowed my lifelong inhibition about letter-writing to prevent me from responding. As time went on, the neglect seemed unforgivable and the unanswered mail sat accusingly on my desk.

One by one I began to reply, aware that *while I was composing the letters to abandoned friends, feelings of my own abandonment evaporated.* Their forgiving responses followed. I was expanding the boundaries of my social world and, in the process, learning that I could sustain a consoling connection even with friends who were out of sight or far away.

My friend Karen enjoys her life on her own after sixteen years of marriage. "At first I was a little lonely, but not nearly as lonely as I'd felt with my unresponsive husband. Believe me, there is no worse loneliness than with an emotionally distant spouse; I was trapped in an ongoing sense of abandonment and felt impotent to change it. Now if I feel lonely I can *do* something about it—choose the company of friends who make me feel welcome.

"It was hard going at first. I'd always been a man's woman and hadn't given much weight to friendships with women, or men with whom there was no romance. I had to learn how to *be* a friend, how to coax friendship into blossoming and follow up caringly. It was hard work. But isn't it funny how we're told to work at marriage but we're not encouraged to work at being alone? And it *is* work! Especially in our mobile society."

Karen was right, it *was* work. After months of labor, feeling particularly vulnerable and, frankly, exhausted from the effort to avoid loneliness, I invited Leo to lunch.

"Why is it," I lamented, "that just when I get my social life together it falls apart on me? Molly moved to

Canada, Lenora went on tour, Steve disappeared into his marriage, Marvin into a depression and Marianne into her work, not to mention watching everyone skip off in August. I feel as if I'm building sand castles that keep getting washed out to sea." Leo looked amused.

"I need more sand," I conceded.

I grumbled to Leo that I seemed to be the one doing all the initiating, inviting and entertaining. People waited for me to arrange the next event. Leo understood my frustration at always being the bridge builder, but he helped me realize that if I could accept this role without resentment, I'd be in a stronger position. At least I'd know I was making the eventual rewards possible.

❧

There were lots of jolts ahead. People would cancel at the last minute or I would forget to plan ahead for a holiday and find myself marooned in solitude. I often succumbed to gloom and routinely grappled with a terrible passivity that defeated any action whatsoever.

In spite of such setbacks, that winter I put together monthly candlelit dinners (Chinese takeout; cooking isn't my thing) with two friends where we would share our favorite poetry or arrange periodic musical evenings for friends to sing together or entertain one another. I hosted a goal group that still meets every six weeks to review each other's progress and a monthly writing group where we share our projects. I labored to tug friends or potential friends into my orbit. I put in *lots* of effort, and eventually the human supplies were not only becoming adequate but spawning others. Little by little my days were sprinkled with endearing friends and acquaintances as well as beautiful artistic and collaborative events.

⁓

I still had to prepare for the inevitable evenings alone, however, so I compiled a list of activities to enjoy on my own: lectures, concerts, art exhibits, movies. At first I felt a little self-conscious attending events alone and tended to study my program instead of making eye contact with so many strangers. But as I practiced observing the group and taking advantage of openings for conversation—say, with a seat mate over a dropped program or when standing in line for coffee at intermission—I discovered we weren't really strangers after all—we were familiars bonded by our mutual interest in the event.

Some evenings I felt happily at home with fellow attendees (with or without conversation) and sometimes I still felt like an orphan, but I staggered on, clinging to my faith that somewhere down the line this would all pay off. It did.

After the long campaign I was finally winning the battle against the dragon of loneliness. I began to feel warmly integrated into the world—even more so than when I was coupled—and felt blessed that living alone had offered me such a life-enriching challenge.

One night, as I was perched in the creamy heights of Carnegie Hall listening to Alfred Brendel play Beethoven, I imagined our earth suspended in the vastness of the universe. I thought, *Here we are, a cluster of humans come together to experience the beauty of music. It's as if all our hearts are joined by invisible threads to that of the artist and together we form one huge heart.*

Lying in bed that night I felt attached to many others out in the world by those same invisible threads. The "barren waste" was retreating; the water was rising from the river in which I'd been standing all along.

Paradoxically, now that I felt the world was connected to me I began to enjoy my days of solitude. It was time to go more deeply into the adventure, but first I needed to attend to some practical business.

REMEMBER THAT BEING BY ONESELF
IS NOT THE SAME AS BEING ABANDONED.
THE WORLD IS STILL THERE.

• *Notice the potential for comfort in the world at large.* Don't be shy. We all have something in common, even if it's only the weather. Speak with tradespeople and neighbors, and with others at a concert, on public transportation or in a museum. Practice courage in initiating contact. Delivery people, bank personnel, doormen are all potential sources of small but significant human encounters. Practice really *seeing* them, really *listening,* really *responding* and welcome the human comfort they offer.

• *Identify diners, coffee houses and restaurants where you're comfortable eating by yourself.* If you feel self-conscious about dining alone, return frequently to favorite restaurants; the familiarity with those who serve you and with other "regulars" should soon overcome it. At first it may feel more comfortable to take along a book, newspaper or notebook as a prop with which to occupy yourself, but eventually you will want to be open to conversation with the staff or perhaps with other patrons. The best subjects are often the universal ones, like the news, or the food, or the changes you may notice in the surroundings.

• *Make a list of "human resources."* This list can include family, close confidants, phone pals, spur-of-the-moment buddies and potential friends. Post it and check it often to make sure it's current and that you're staying in touch. If you haven't heard from one of your friends lately don't assume that he or she has forgotten about you; it probably has nothing to do with you. Pick up the phone and leave a message that you're thinking of him or her. Be sure that you've cultivated an ample number of friends and are staying open to new relationships. This will be insurance against your social structure being too depleted when someone moves away and will be a check on demanding too much of any one person.

• *Build bridges.* Be the one to arrange to have meals with others either at home or in a restaurant. Stay aware of events you can attend with friends: sports, film, theater, concerts, carnivals. Be willing to make the calls, order the tickets, gather transportation information. Host a gathering each month to share some common interest: books, cards, movies, music. Embrace the role of the

barbara feldon

bridge builder; it's the best way to establish a rewarding social circle.

• *Cultivate e-mail and handwritten correspondence.* It's a casual and convenient way to deepen friendships or develop new ones and can become a daily source of fun and immediate gratification. Try to answer written notes promptly in order to encourage the exchange. (To make it more convenient, perhaps set aside a portion of your desk for stationery and envelopes.) Notice the pleasure of communicating with those who are out of sight or far away as you share in their lives and interests.

• *Identify activities that draw you into the community and participate in them.* Scan the newspaper or the Internet each week for local events. This is your community and you want to be part of it. There are town hall meetings, important hearings, street associations and historical societies. There may be photography and art exhibits, local opera groups and community theater productions, all of which express the energy and talent of neighbors. Join a church group, bowling or other sports teams, an art or cooking class, a chorale society, a literary society. By attending and showing interest you can participate in your community in a way that could lead to a deeper involvement in the future.

Get a list of volunteer opportunities from your local chamber of commerce, League of Women Voters, coalitions for the homeless, hospitals, churches, the YMCA, YWCA or YMHA, Girls Incorporated or schools. Nothing is more comforting than reaching out in ways that comfort others.

• *Protect yourself on holidays.* Holidays are not the time to be stoic. No matter how smoothly you're sailing along on your own, major holidays are white water if you haven't prepared for them in advance. Try to be with family, friends or at a social gathering even if you fear it will be boring; boredom is better than feeling bereft. Traveling with a group can also be a way to experience the holiday as a vacation. If all else fails, attend a public event or serve dinner at a homeless shelter.

• *Enroll in a college extension program.* Our minds are eager for intellectual thrills and living alone affords us the time to seek them. Most learning institutes have adult extension programs—often at night—that offer courses in almost anything. Phone them or check their

Web site to obtain a brochure listing their curriculum and enroll, either alone or with a friend. Pick endeavors that will challenge you for the rest of your life, perhaps music, art, writing or literature. This is a great way to open yourself to new pursuits or deepen old ones and an opportunity to meet people with interests compatible to yours.

• *Join a gym, yoga class or dance class.* Those who feel too depleted by evening to engage in intense hobbies, social activities or intellectual interests might want to join a gym to work off some of the day's tension in the company of others. The meditative aspects of yoga can add a spiritual dimension to your life and a ballroom dance class can offer the sheer joy of moving to music with others.

• *Stop believing that marriage is the solution to loneliness.* It is easier to jettison this idea if you've been half of a failed couple and can remember the pain of daily alienation. Seeking escape from loneliness is a dangerous reason to be coupled. It's best to solve the loneliness issue on your own as insurance against dragging it into a future relationship. Create an environment of social and self-support that can protect you from forming inappropriate relationships based solely on need.

• *Let go of the idea that someone else can make your life wonderful.* Your happiness is in your own hands; that's the safest place for it.

The mind is its own place,
can make a heav'n of hell, a
—JOHN MILTON

banishing
negative thinking

(we each have a tolerance level for solitude
that is important to recognize in order
to prevent a flood of distress)

During the first few weeks of living on my own—
spending unaccustomed time alone and bereft of the validation of romance—I crashed in on myself and became
plagued by negative thoughts. The bathroom mirror
became the silver screen on which I starred in my very

horror film. Every flaw, overlooked in the reassuring glow of a relationship, became inflated in solitude. Good God! How did that little crow's foot deepen into the Grand Canyon? I would approach the mirror intending to brush my teeth and stagger away convicted by its evidence. Of course, I was helped down this dreary road by seeing a cosmetic ad in my Playbill one evening at the theater. A famous model was sprawled gorgeously on a chaise under the caption "You too can be sexy. Even after thirty." I was newly living alone and rather seriously "after thirty."

Negative thinking never bit into me when I was working or in the company of friends, but after long hours alone I would be bombarded by doomy thoughts. I was surprised to realize *there is a tolerance level for solitude that is important to recognize in order to prevent a flood of distress*. I learned either to honor it, or to neglect it at my peril. I could trot along for a time delighting in solitude, then, like the cartoon character who skips out into thin air unaware that there's nothing beneath him until he looks down, I would suddenly find myself at the bottom of a pit entangled in melancholy.

The wreckage was compounded by the idea that *devoid of a man I'd failed at being a woman*. I'd inhaled this concept at my mother's knee (she didn't have to teach it, she lived it). It was the very air I breathed—that many of us still breathe—and was as unnoticed and lethal as poison gas.

Once I discovered gloomy thinking, I began to practice "creative negativity" and even got quite good at it. One night I went alone to a restaurant, settled into my chair and was about to read the menu when I focused on a couple across the room. They were holding hands in the candlelight and gazing rapturously into each other's eyes. Yearning surged through me; they embodied perfect love! The great prize! The thing I lacked! Never mind that on occasion I had been half of a candlelit couple myself, and that the passion I displayed then was in inverse proportion to the longevity of the relationship. I was instantly tossed back to high school.

Up popped Betty Ann Rankin—who had beat me out for the cheerleading squad—in the klieg lights of the football stadium on that crisp September night of the playoffs with Baldwin High. Bouncing at halftime in front of the cheering crowd she demonstrated her perfect legs and frisky bosoms while exchanging secret signals with the linebacker, Charlie Benton, my heartthrob but her boyfriend. I watched enviously while shivering on a hard bleacher clutching my cold hot dog and lukewarm Coke.

I resurrected this memory (do we ever recover from high school?) in the moment of observing the romantic couple in the restaurant. I slunk home weighted by deprivation and self-doubt.

Then came the dank 3 A.M. ruminations on flopped relationships and the threat of being alone forever. Out there in the world, I thought, people are nested against each other in coupled lives that hum along happily while mine is beached in devastation. Another torture was hooking my thoughts to the dread of death with its black-hooded finality, clanging the chains of eternity.

I needed to view myself and my situation differently.

But old traditions die hard. I once read about a team of engineers who went to a remote part of Africa to teach farmers how to lay pipes for irrigation. The farmers first watched a demonstration film, then they were tested on how much information they'd absorbed.

"What did you see in the film?" they were asked.

Farmer after farmer answered, "The chickens. We saw the chickens."

"The chickens? What chickens?" The engineers were

puzzled and reran the footage to see what the farmers were talking about. During the course of the film chickens could be seen running around on a hill in the distance. The farmers had simply focused on what they were accustomed to seeing.

If I were persisting in stigmatizing myself for living alone, then I was still seeing chickens!

It was helpful to see a therapist to discover that, among other things, I was resisting becoming responsible for myself. *Dependency had been delicious candy, but it was habit forming and left me feeling insecure without it. I needed to give it up and mourn its loss.* Only then, like a caring "self-mother," could I have compassion for myself and begin to grow.

❧

Understanding the roots of my negativity was only the first step. Every day I had to muster the will to battle against negative thoughts and try to substitute a positive view of myself. Sometimes the right tool just falls in your lap. One night as I was rearranging my bookshelves I came across an old, heavily underlined copy of dialogues with the Indian teacher J. Krishnamurti. I opened it idly and noticed a passage I had starred three times. He was attempting to convince a man to give up seeing the world in a negative light. "But," the man protested, "how can I? I had a childhood . . ." Krishnamurti interrupted him, "Sir, simply stop it!" I laughed out loud at this blunt prescription, wrote it on a Post-it and stuck it to my mirror. From then on every time I threatened myself with a negative thought I would apply the imperative: *"Simply stop it!"* When it worked I felt as if I were a goalie preventing the pucks of negativity from scoring. It was an arduous game but I've never improved on that defense.

Once we *defuse our personal arsenal of negative material,* what can we do about society's grading system that gives us a gold star for being married and low marks for being single?

Have we failed if we don't have a partner? Will we be abandoned if we don't have children or a mate? Is there salvation in romance? Are we actually undesirable after a certain age? (I've noticed that some other cultures are more inclined to regard men and women as attractive no matter what their age, proportions or marital status. I was heartened when I met Pam, my first mentor, who, living alone in London at fifty-something—and not slender—was filled with self-respect and greatly admired by her friends as an attractive and, frankly, sexual woman.) Although these ideas have been disproven in practice they continue to smolder beneath "enlightened" rhetoric, waiting to exert their negative influence.

There is no "right" road, but there is a map of possibilities that we are free to explore in many directions. Our challenge is to *take a stand against outdated attitudes. If we regard our single status as inferior to being married, then the problem is in ourselves.* And when we look in the mirror and are dismayed at our image, it is helpful to understand that *we* are reinforcing society's distorted messages every time we see ourselves as an age or a body and not as a *person*.

We each have a closet full of favored negative thoughts that we can don or shed anytime we choose. And it *is* a choice once we have examined their origins and discredited them. The trick is to "simply stop" them in their tracks and think more kindly of ourselves.

ACKNOWLEDGE YOUR RESPONSIBILITY FOR BANISHING NEGATIVE THOUGHTS.

• *Try to understand the underlying causes of mentally attacking yourself.* This might be done with a therapist, a friend or by self-examination in a journal. The loss of a reassuring relationship may trigger negativity that has been lying dormant for years. It is important to discover its origins—perhaps in childhood—to diminish its power in your adult life. To avoid reinforcing those negative thoughts, try to "simply stop" them as they rise up to plague you. Meditation is an excellent method. By focusing your attention on your breath or an object, you can begin to gently dismiss disturbing thoughts as they arise. Another exercise is to practice looking at each negative issue from different angles and list several different ways of viewing it. For example, if you are obsessing about being rejected, list those people in your life who welcome and accept you.

• *Question the cultural prejudice of viewing marriage as the only road to happiness.* Assess the world with new eyes to determine what will realistically lead to a fulfilling life.

Think of examples that prove old ideas about living alone to be mistaken. For example, list people you know who enjoy living on their own, those who have chosen it, those whose lives are happy without the validation of a partner and those who have no mate or kids and still feel secure.

Try to live outside cultural prejudices as though you were living in a foreign land by projecting more enlightened values; be aware of negative messages and refuse to apply them to yourself.

• *Don't depend on a partner for your self-esteem.* Never give away your value to someone else. If you've been in a dependent relationship, you might be especially prone to do this. It's important to wean yourself from the approval of another person.

Create a pool of validation sources: friends, your work, your talent. For example, recall your successful endeavors—projects at which you've excelled, community contributions you've made, friendships you've forged. Mastering a skill or a sport is also a good way to develop a sense of autonomy, accomplishment and self-esteem, essentials for living alone happily. Concentrate on your achievements, not on your failings.

• *Avoid criticizing your body or viewing aging as an embarrassment.* Each time you do, you're perpetuating the societal distortion. Try to see that you are adequate as you are. You aren't an age or a body but a *person.* Don't buy into advertising that is promoting a product at the expense of your self-esteem or movies that present an idealized view of what is lovable. Become aware of those who don't have perfect bodies or who are no longer in the first blush of youth and still find the world responding to them as valuable and sensual individuals.

• *Become your own best ally, not your worst enemy.* Intervene as a good friend would if you begin to sink into negative thoughts about yourself or your situation. Don't believe in your negative self-assessments. Remember that you have viewed yourself positively under different circumstances—rekindle those attitudes now. Recall the positive things that people have said to you and give them precedence over your negative self-view. Be supportive of your efforts to take care of yourself and be tolerant of backsliding.

Write down all the things that would be good for your life. Star those that would give you the most pleasure and resolve to carry them out. Be sure to include something pleasurable each day: a special meal, entertainment, a good book, conversation with friends.

• *Stop dwelling on events and people who have disappointed you.* It's easy to review past slights and betrayals or gnaw on career failures. Sometimes it's helpful to write down all your grievances, put them in a drawer and close it. It's important to be *determined* to stop torturing yourself and act accordingly. For each negative memory, try to substitute a recollection of those people who have come through for you.

• *Avoid negative thinkers because they reinforce your fears.* If an acquaintance persists in focusing on the misery of being alone or aging or laments constantly about his or her appearance, notice whether this person's negativity is undermining your confidence. Chances are it is, especially when you are first mastering the art of living alone. It may be helpful to avoid seeing these people in situations where they are free to vent. Cultivate positive, active people with enthusiastic natures who regard life as a gift whether one is partnered or single. Remember, attitudes are contagious.

• *Pay attention to your level of tolerance for solitude.* Experiment with time alone and observe the point at which pleasurable solitude becomes uncomfortable or when you begin to feel anxious or start down a negative mental path. Protect yourself, especially on holidays, from the results of pushing the solitary envelope. When you are newly alone be especially aware of your need for company and don't overestimate your solitude tolerance level. Trying to master it too fast isn't productive when you are most vulnerable. It's helpful to plan your week, balancing alone time with social contact.

• *Make a list of your favorite negative thoughts.* We all have a cupboard full. Do you usually pick on your looks, intelligence, single status, career? If you can name them and understand what triggers them, they will begin to lose their power. Know your enemy as though you are planning for an invasion; determine when and where they are likely to attack and be ready to refute their messages.

As sharp as in my childhood, still
Ecstasy shocks me fixed.
—EDNA ST. VINCENT MILLAY

intimacy

(living alone gives us the freedom to
nourish the things we love without the
constraints of a partner's timetable or
his or her conflicting desires)

Intimacy is that blissful feeling of absorption in another
where nothing is missing. As infants we find it in our
mother's embrace; as adults we seek it in the arms of a
lover. Poets rhapsodize about the oasis of passion where
the world dissolves, time holds its breath and lovers in
self-surrender feel they are one with each other and complete at last.

When I was first without a relationship I felt a poignant sense of missing something and sought to coax a man into my orbit again to "complete" me. Happily, my romantic fortunes faltered long enough for me to discover that intimacy is not exclusive to love; it can be found in surprising places. In fact, *we are intimate with anything to which we surrender our whole being*.

❧

In 1983, at age eighty-one, Barbara McClintock won the Nobel prize for her research into the genes of corn. In an interview she said, "As you look at these things they become part of you. And you forget yourself." Then she spoke of *"the real affection"* one gets for the pieces of the puzzle that "go together." It struck me that she was using the language of love. In the moments McClintock surrendered herself to the jumping genes—*became part of them*—she felt there was nothing missing in her life. I realized that her intimacy with the genes wasn't a substitute for love; that *romantic love is only one of many ways to be intimate*.

Of course, intimacy's primary home is in the rich communion we share with others. I remember one night dining with a friend at a candlelit table by the Boating Pond in Central Park. As we tossed ideas back and forth our response to each other was as intense and concentrated as a musical duet. All personal concerns and even the magic of the New York skyline twinkling through the trees dissolved in the closeness of our exchange. I felt bonded, complete; nothing was missing.

But what about the days when human connection is unavailable? Such times are familiar to those who live alone. How do we find our version of Barbara McClintock's jumping genes? In other words, *how can we engage ourselves passionately?*

ᶜᵛ

One day when I was in second grade, Mother realized that neither she nor my older sister would be there when I came home from school. Anticipating my misery she asked my sister, Pat, to write out a series of arithmetic problems on a little yellow pad to distract me until she arrived. That afternoon I walked into the empty house and the yellow pad lay glowing on the dining room table as if it were in a spotlight, a pencil poised carefully on top. I carried it like a sacred object onto the front porch, settled into a chair's plastic uphol-stery and began adding the columns of figures. The threat of a lonely afternoon receded as the world of arithmetic charmed me with numerical magic. *I was so absorbed that I was aware of nothing missing, not even Mother. It was my first adventure into sublimation.* The arithmetic had become associated with Mother, yet offered satisfactions even she could not provide.

I experienced that "nothing missing" bliss again during my first ballet lesson when I was twelve. Jean Ralph—shorts, high heels, blue eye shadow—lined me up with three other girls and handed us each a paper fan. Then she showed us how to make a T with our feet and said it was called third position.

"Now girls," she said, "when I start the music I want you to make a big arc with your arm and pass your fan to the next girl."

I felt awkward and insecure—still carrying what my mother called "baby fat." But then Jean walked to the phonograph, placed the needle on the record and unleashed the sweetness of the *Nutcracker Suite*. As my arm rose in an arc, the music seemed to be rising from within me as though some angel presence had awak-ened and was ascending in splendor, transporting me to a realm I hadn't known existed but that felt like my true home.

Throughout high school, dance lifted me above the storms of adolescence, but college conflicted with my training and by the time I graduated it was too late to pursue my dancing aspirations. Then for many years afterward the distractions of career and relationships occupied all my waking hours, and though my life often felt incomplete, I didn't have much time to worry about it.

Once I was living on my own and was awash with harshly empty hours, I realized something extraordinary was painfully missing. The enthralling experiences of the past had been put aside for so long that they seemed like distant siren songs. There was nothing about which I felt passionately. I needed a connection to something that profoundly interested me but I didn't know how to find it, until I met Daniel.

Daniel, a poet in his forties, owned a printing company, enjoyed an active social life and had lived alone for thirteen years. The night we met I was stunned to learn that, even though he had a full-time job, he managed to spend five hours a day reading. Daniel didn't just read, he plunged into literature, dove into its depths, bathed in it, relished it! "Good God," I thought. "Reading five hours a day? Is that *allowed*?" In childhood I'd experienced the rapture of being absorbed in a book, but as an adult I felt guilty if I read for very long when I could be "doing something productive." The notion of reading for the heady sake of reading as opposed to something one does after sweating the important things like accumulating money or making a mark in the world seemed dangerously anarchic.

I decided to become an anarchist.

When I told Daniel that I loved to read but didn't know how to find the great books, he looked at me with the expression of someone about to rescue a lost puppy. From his jacket pocket he pulled out a notebook and pen, scribbled down a number of book titles, thrust the list at me and said, "Start with these." Too intimidated to refuse, I set about working my way through the list, which started with Homer and proceeded through other classics. Doors within me flew open; I rediscovered the bliss that I hadn't pursued beyond my childhood. I feasted on books, was drunk on them. I read till four in the morning, I read while eating, while traveling. Once I survived the tedium of a twelve-hour flight involving two layovers by surrendering to the world of Marcel

Proust, barely glancing up from his words even while walking through terminals. He transported me from the cold practicality of the Dallas airport to a summer-fragrant resort in turn-of-the-century France. The twentieth century disappeared as his world became my temporary home, a complete home where nothing was missing.

Proust said we read to know ourselves; there are many more selves to know than can come to light in our ordinary lives. When we and the writer meet on the page our silent communion crosses centuries. The author, like a caring guide, shares his or her deepest thoughts and feelings, and if we are openhearted readers, some wall within us will crumble allowing our unsuspected selves to flicker to life. Without us the writer's words would be meaningless, without the writer we would be stranded in half-lives. Inside each book a warm-blooded human being is reaching out to us, and whether we are being entertained or enlightened we are never alone while reading.

As one book led to the next and my own list sprouted from Daniel's, shock after shock of self-recognition passed through me like electrical yesses. Like a collaborator I underlined—even in ink—passages that spoke to me and that I wanted to revisit. It was no longer the writer's book, it was *our* book.

Aside from reading, I wondered, what other interest might I resurrect? I dug back through my adult rubble and remembered the ecstasy of listening to music. I began attending concerts. Succumbing to the world of sound in the community of others gave me some of the most sacred moments of my life, bypassing my consciousness and touching my heart. Not only was nothing missing, the moments were overflowing; when I left the concert halls I always felt larger, more complete than when I had entered.

Then I remembered singing in the high school chorus, experiencing the bliss of harmony. I decided to study voice, but no sooner had that thought flashed into my head than it was injured by an old resistance to attempting anything new. A tingle of paralysis crept through me. I was booted out of this condition by my friend Jean, a musician who had recently divorced.

"I'd always wanted to form a string quartet," she said, "but after my divorce I was draped around the apartment so mired in gloom that I couldn't mobilize myself. Of course, it's important to mourn for a time and work through the loss, but I realized at a certain point that I was sunk in passivity. Then one day I got out a Magic Marker, a piece of poster board and wrote in big black letters 'DO IT!' and propped it on my bureau. Every morning when I woke up, it sat there like an admonishing teacher. It was tough love but it worked!"

I took her advice and wrote "Do it!" (on a filing card out of deference to decor) and posted it on my bathroom mirror. Did it work? Well, sort of. I could "Do it" if I could just stop cleaning closets, rearranging furniture and eroding my time with other meaningless chores. In order to get beyond these procrastinations, I had to break the process of studying singing into a series of simple tasks; call a friend who sings to get her referral of a teacher. *Do it!* Make an appointment for a lesson. Pick up the phone. *Do it!* Go to the library, research and photo- copy the music I want to sing. *Do it!* So I did.

I found an enthusiastic teacher who nudged me into singing operatic arias, not in order to storm the Met, but for the sheer thrill of it. The emotional *excess* of music felt more real than the muted emotion and soft demeanor I expressed in daily life. When I was this pas- sionately engaged I didn't need anything else to "complete" me; not a man, not career affirmation. I only had to give in to the music to live an immense life that I could experience any time I chose.

I knew I could never perfect the art of singing, but sometimes our most thrilling endeavors are those that, though they defy mastery, coax us into deeper levels of ourselves. Jan Stussy, my artist friend, told me that we must "intensify the search," meaning we should reach more deeply into our interests and offer them as much devotion and surrender as we would to a lover. To find those interests requires enormous curiosity and the wish—as the psychoanalyst Erich Fromm has put it—to be *fully born*.

Passionate interests have the potential to cross-pollinate. Years ago I met a woman who was fascinated by the history of bread. "If you study bread," she told me, "eventually you learn everything about the society that made it; who tilled the fields, who harvested the grain, the artists who created the utensils and the art that adorns them, the status of women, farmers and merchants, even their economy." It seems that if you pick up the thread of almost any interest and are eager to follow it, it can weave together the whole world!

Lucia lives by herself in a house tucked into a hillside of pine trees. She works at a hospital all day, then at night she comes home and plunges into opera. Not opera as background music to her evening meal, but opera as a gateway into a wilder world of emotions than her clinical work permits. In turn, this has led her to a fascination with the history of opera and the lives of the composers and singers, which has enlivened her interest in other artists of the time as well as the history and politics of the countries where they lived. Like a cell that keeps dividing itself, Lucia's love of opera has spawned a colony of other fascinations that have brought greater depth to her single life.

Buddy, a sports enthusiast who lives alone, talks about baseball in much the same way.

"When I'm watching baseball," he told me, "I have no sense of being alone. I'm with those guys on the field completely absorbed in every play. I'm inside it, totally filled with the intensity of the game. Baseball's philosophy: It teaches you that anything can still happen, that you need never give up. It's psychology: Can the pitcher maintain his composure under pressure? Can the batter? Can the team hold itself together? It's strategy and nuance: the way each ball is thrown and why. It's human nature: How do the players conduct their lives? Its possibilities are beautiful moment to moment."

Buddy is not simply interested in baseball, he is enthralled with it. Baseball has brought him some of the most profoundly "nothing missing" hours of his life.

I like to think that developing deep interests is similar to fishing, trolling with a number of lines in the water and hauling in surprising species. Scientists have shown that the mind grows by surprises. Put simply, when something new sparks our interest an aperture forms in some outpost of the brain, gulps down an enzyme and sprouts a branch that can actually be measured. Imagine the orchards that are cultivated in our brains as we embrace new experiences and pursue with passion those interests that once attracted us but have been sadly mislaid along the way.

Posi, a school counselor in Indiana, found herself with an empty nest after her children went out into the world, followed immediately by her defecting husband. Once she had suffered through the divorce, she began to survey her life, focusing on the things she had never pursued but that had always intrigued her. At the top of her list was tap dancing. She wasn't alone—a local judge shared her fancy, and they put together a group of five women who attend tap class each week, then retire to a coffee shop for good conversation. It's the best day of their week. Though they've resisted donning spangled costumes and tapping in public, they continue, after four years, to enrich their friendships through the exhilaration of dance.

⁓

Obviously, anyone can develop interests, so what does this have to do with living alone? *Living alone gives us the freedom to nourish the things we love without the constraints of a partner's timetable or his or her conflicting desires.* We are free to grow in our unique direction if we pursue those things that excite us, touch our hearts and make us feel fully alive.

I like to imagine having interests so varied that we might hop from one to another at will during any lull in our normal activities. Whenever we wish, a door opens to reveal more doors to other rooms within us, whether they be rooms of music, conversation, gardening, sports or inventing the widget. And though some activities must be indulged in solitude, we are never alone when we engage in them. We find joy in the unseen company of authors, composers, sports figures, even the jumping genes in corn!

It's never too late to cultivate interests. When Socrates was seventy and in prison waiting to drink the hemlock, he heard of a man who was traveling through Athens teaching the lyre. He said to a friend, "Bring him to me. I've always wanted to learn to play that instrument."

His friend said, "But Socrates, you're going to be dead in three days."

Socrates replied, "Yes, but I have three days to learn it!"

IDENTIFY THOSE THINGS THAT DEEPLY ENGROSS
YOU, THAT MAKE YOU FEEL COMPLETE, THAT
MAKE YOU FEEL AS THOUGH NOTHING IS MISSING.
ENCOURAGE YOURSELF TO "DO IT!"

• *Search back through your childhood or the last time you were single for clues to interests that may have attracted you but were laid aside.* For example, you may have wanted to play the guitar, write poetry, conduct a band, become a chef, form a salon, play the piano. *Be bold.* Try not to worry about what others will think—you alone are inside your soul and know what will bring you the greatest satisfaction and make you feel fully alive. Be acutely aware of the things you enjoy and have always wanted to do. Don't dismiss an interest because you think it's too late to start. Remember, Socrates wanted to learn to play the lyre three days before his execution!

• *Write down each action you must take in order to pursue your interest.* If you'd like to play the piano, for example: *a.* Decide on the kind of teacher that would best serve you: basic technique, jazz, pop, classical. *b.* Compile a list of appropriate teachers referred by piano-playing friends or college music departments. *c.* Contact each in order of preference to determine their schedule, fee and location. *d.* Arrange a meeting. *e.* Collect the music needed. *f.* Plan a practice schedule. *g.* Set time goals for the mastery of each piece. *h.* When you've reached a certain level of mastery, plan regular evenings with other musical friends to share your love of music and entertain one another.

Check off each of these steps as you take them. When you feel yourself procrastinating or feeling discouraged, make a note of your reasons for resistance, and try to understand them. Finally, encourage yourself to simply *Do it!* This start-up stage of developing activities is the hardest, so don't be discouraged if you find yourself resisting the process. It's human. Keep in mind that there are rewards ahead, including the self-respect you will gain from persevering.

• *Go more deeply into your existing interests.* The depth of your commitment turns a casual interest into a passionate one. For example, if your interest is gardening, extend it beyond your backyard. Join a botanical society or garden club, or take a course on formal gardens at a local college. There are garden-viewing tours to Europe and a wealth of great literature on the subject. You may extend your interest in flowers to greenhouse gardening in the winter. Some people become fascinated with flower arranging or the medicinal properties of plants. It's astonishing how rich, wide-ranging and exciting a subject can be. Don't be satisfied with the surface. Dig deeper; that's where the magic lies.

• *Be open to a wide range of new experiences.* The more lines you have in the water, the greater the possibility of catching something remarkable. Welcome the opportunity if a friend asks you to sit in on his or her painting class, take a chance on enrolling in a cooking class or ballroom dancing class, sign up for a lecture series, take recommendations of and read books that you hadn't considered. Take advantage of the time and freedom that living alone allows you to sample and experiment with a variety of things that might eventually interest you passionately. Remember, interests spawn interests.

• *Choose interests that are compatible with your time and energy constraints.* If your job is physically exhausting, instead of dancing you might prefer listening to music or reading. If you feel mentally depleted from studying documents all day, a sculpture or sketch class might be refreshing, or perhaps try a stimulating conversation with a friend. Try to be selective about viewing television. Though TV has interesting things to see from time to time, it can sabotage your wish to dive deeply into interests that have much more to offer you in the long run. It's hard to attain that "nothing-missing" feeling on a steady diet of television.

• *Seek out others with similar interests and arrange to meet regularly.* If your common interest is writing, you might form a writing group and meet once a month at someone's home to share your work or favorite authors with one another. Classes are a great way to meet colleagues as well as garden clubs, literary and music societies and seminars. Along the way you may be making enduring friendships.

• *Post the reminder "Do it!" in a place where you will see it every day.*

And stand together yet not too near together:
For the pillars of the temple stand apart,
And the oak tree and the cypress grow
not in each other's shadow.
—KAHLIL GIBRAN

and what of romance?

(living alone has its own charms and
opportunities for connection different
from marriage, yet it need never be
a romantic wasteland)

Are we forever exiled from love if we live alone?

Almost certainly not if we want it. But a 3 A.M. fear
shivers through the newly alone (or soon to be solo)
romantics when they contemplate life without being

entwined nightly with a beloved. Surely we're meant to mate and no one would willingly pass up the bliss that nature has bestowed on love. But the anguish often associated with being without a romantic connection seems overheated; like orphans starving in a snowstorm, singles sometimes feel excluded from the perfect feast they imagine others devouring.

But a love life is not a *need* like food and air, it's a *desire*. If we don't eat or breathe, we die; we don't die from unsatisfied passion. *Having to set aside romance from time to time is only tormenting if we choose to view it that way.* Being without a partner can be—and often is—experienced as a desolate condition, but there is a more positive and, yes, enjoyable way to explore it.

Rosemary, a therapist who sees a number of single patients, told me that each one deals with his or her love life (or lack of it) differently: "Mating is one of life's deepest delights but only one, sexual energy (George Bernard Shaw called it 'the life force'), can be deflected onto a variety of other kinds of human connection. It can be poured into artistic pursuits, or into one's work, and some singles enjoy the titillation of romance in romance novels. (A publisher once told me that if you piled up all the romance novels read in one day they would reach to the top of the Empire State Building.) Some people I work with who live alone for long periods without a relationship find that, yes, they have sexual yearnings from time to time, but when they focus on what they *can* have and cultivate those pleasures, the longing becomes quiescent and untroubling—but not dead. When romance is again in the vicinity, their desire springs into the foreground as fresh as ever.

"For those without a partner," she continued, "society's message that the only way to be happy is to be mated causes the pain of sexual envy. Singles often imagine they're deprived of some fabulous love others are enjoying. It's not a bad idea to realistically flick a bit of stardust off the 'ideal' of romance to reduce the sense of loss when it eludes us. How many couples actually find the movie version of perfect love? Did the movie stars themselves? Married passion surely exists, but it's certainly not inevitable."

I was reminded of a night I was watching the Academy Awards alone. When the male star won the Oscar for best performance, he lifted it in tribute to his wife in the audience and professed his love. As the camera caught her tear-streaked face and adoring eyes I felt a stab of envy and thought I would give anything to trade places with her. A few months later they were divorced. *It's not so much what we're missing—it's what we fantasize we're missing.*

That's not to say that romance isn't possible or that we shouldn't wish for and pursue it. *We're dreaming creatures and it would be untrue to our natures if we gave up our yearnings.* Living alone provides time to explore our dreams and they *can* be fulfilled, if not exactly as the movies portray, in satisfying if sometimes unconventional ways.

During the first few months of living on my own I was so habituated to being part of a love relationship I undervalued "lesser" connections with men who were merely pals and pursued an intense but painfully uncommitted involvement. Parallel to this ill-fated affair I formed a friendship with Jan, an artist to whom I confessed the roller-coaster dips and peaks of my love life and commiserated with (or applauded) his romantic fortunes. Although Jan and I lived a great distance from each other, we made audiotapes almost daily sharing our thoughts and our interest in poetry. We flew off to Ireland on vacations to hunt sacred Celtic stones and to southern Mexico to explore the ruins of Palenque. My boyfriend tolerated my excursions with Jan, certain that the friendship we shared was purely platonic. And it was. Sort of. True, there was no overt sexual chemistry between us; in fact, we were so untempted by each other that we would share a room as chastely as siblings. And yet, when I recall my most romantic memories from that decade they are never of the man with whom I was "in love." They are of Jan: walking together beneath towering trees on a misty night in Ireland; a music-filled Mexican restaurant in Mérida where we defined for ourselves the meaning of life (to live intensely); or the night in Holland, standing on a cliff overlooking the North Sea watching swans glide through a ribbon of moonlight.

I learned that *there are ways to experience romance outside of sexual possession.* I had savored for the first time what the sixteenth-century essayist Montaigne called "passionate friendship": one that is deeply loving, unconditional and heightened to the level of poetry. We delighted in each other's company, expressed ourselves freely, and brought out the best in each other. Not all conventional relationships can make those claims. There were so many delights that the lack of a sexual component wasn't felt as a deficit.

e❧

"You'll always have men in your life if you want them," a friend once told me, "even if you never find the perfect partner. Perhaps instead of having one man you'll have several who together will equal one man."

I felt a shock of hope. I knew he didn't mean promiscuity; he was a champion of fidelity. He was suggesting that I venture outside my habit of attaching my affection to only one person and develop ties with more than one man—even from different generations—with whom I could share various aspects of myself and who together would add up to a "relationship" that would be fulfilling in its own way. It was an exciting idea; if no prince ever found my slipper, there were other ways to enjoy that special cello tone that's set humming when I'm with a man.

Over the years I've treasured friendships with several men—the youngest is twenty-six, the oldest ninety-two—with whom I've enjoyed some of the most heartwarming hours of my life. And though they aren't romantic in the conventional sense, they are not without that unique energy exchange that flows between a man and woman when they enjoy each other's company. Love relationships have come and gone, but the delightful bonds I have with these men have endured.

Aside from sublimation into friendship, those who live alone have found as many solutions to and fulfillments of sexual desire as there are fingerprints. Their styles range from celibacy to *Sex and the City,* depending on their age and personal standards.

Elizabeth, for example, at age forty, has enjoyed an occasional encounter with attractive partners who are not necessarily candidates for lasting relationships. Since she and her lovers are usually friends and both understand the ground rules, she's been able to keep her emotional balance while engaging in spontaneous intimacy.

"These special evenings satisfy my longing for affection and remind me, in a lovely way, that I'm a woman," she said.

Marvin, on the other hand, who took full advantage of the sexual revolution during the seventies, had an experience that caused a sudden about-face.

"I got up in the middle of the night to get a drink of water," he said, "and while I was out of the room I realized with horror that I couldn't remember who was in my bed. I suddenly recognized how empty I felt, that I had confused sex with intimacy and what I really wanted was a deep connection. Now I'm only intimate with a woman if I really care for her and think it might go somewhere."

❧

The truth is, the concept of love has changed dizzyingly from decade to decade, including the idealized love of the forties, the nuclear families of the fifties, the sexual revolution of the sixties and seventies, the AIDS constraints of the eighties, the body-perfect couplings of the nineties and now electronic partnering. How do we blaze our own trail through this thicket of religious beliefs, ethical standards, morality and personal needs? Since there seems to be no universal guide (except practicing safe sex), each of us, by necessity, is on his or her own.

Some singles have intense serial relationships (a friend defined an affair as a relationship that doesn't work out); others have long-standing commitments but prefer to live separately. Patricia, who was widowed as a young woman and has since lived alone in an ocean-side town on the West Coast, occasionally spends time with a man with whom she's been involved for years but who lives a continent away.

"It's great when he visits but I'm not the least bit interested in living with him or with anyone. Since he also enjoys having his own place and needs to live abroad, this arrangement works out well for both of us. We love each other and have an enduring attachment and things are just fine as they are."

Some singles live quite happily without a love object in their lives. Bonnie told me, "There's so much emphasis put on sex but that's never been the important thing for me. It was always the person himself, our closeness emotionally and intellectually as well as sexually. When I was involved and enjoying regular love-making I couldn't imagine my life without it. I was surprised to realize that when I'm not involved with anyone and therefore not expecting intimacy, I rarely give it a thought. I have a lot of interests and really enjoy my life, my friends, my work. When I see a romantic movie I'll remember, yes, how lovely, and I know I'd enjoy being in love again but, frankly, since there's no one I'm interested in, I don't at all suffer from the lack of it."

Being alone doesn't mean you'll never again have love in your life. Since we can trust nature to get men and women together, every day opens a new possibility of finding a partner, perhaps unexpectedly. My friend Edna, who happily lived alone well into her forties, went on an African safari by herself and met an American artist whom she married the following year. A friend's father, Harold, moved into a retirement home and, at eighty-two, found romance. Another friend was so determined to get married that she approached it like an executive starting up a business. She phoned every pal, acquaintance and colleague and announced her willingness to date, at least once, any man they could scare up; his looks were not an issue. It took a couple of years but she did meet and marry someone she considers her perfect partner. *They say if you want love badly enough there's usually a way—at any age—to find it.* Of course, if romance culminates in marriage you'll no longer be living alone. Unless you can afford separate housing. My friend Bob has had a devoted relationship with Ann Marie for thirty years. It is, in every way, as conventional as any marriage with one exception: They live next door to each other. Neither can imagine a better situation.

❧

If you're a romantic there is a protective advantage to living alone. A significant other is among the marvels of life, but not every contender can offer a Shangri-la of fulfillment. Romance may lead to love, but not necessarily. Living alone provides the guardrails of friends and inner autonomy as insurance against losing oneself in that first delirium of infatuation and prematurely surrendering to a relationship you might later regret. With this foundation of strength you can choose a partner for reasons other than need, and set him or her free if it is necessary.

Another element of romance, sensuality, has a broader vocabulary than sex. Whether holding a friend's hand or enjoying a massage, there is a deeply human pleasure to being touched. It would be a shame, especially for those who live alone, to forgo the sensual pampering of bathing in special oils, delectable meals, the tactile pleasure of comfortable bedding; things we very busy Americans tend to neglect.

But what about our deepest concern: How can living alone compare with the exquisite benediction of marriage at its best? It doesn't try to. *Living alone has its own charms and opportunities for connection different from marriage, yet it need never be a romantic wasteland.* True, we may not be wrapped around a loved one every night, but there are cherished encounters that can surprise us at any moment with their flavor of romance if we think outside conventions and embrace them. Whether sex, romance and love are combined or explored separately, living alone gives us the autonomy to tailor them to our lives in individual ways that will bring each of us the greatest joy. Our romantic nature is one of the dearest aspects of being human. Whether it is expressed directly in mating or sublimated in friendship, affection, fantasy or art, it deserves to be celebrated and encouraged to take wing.

LIVING ALONE HAS ITS OWN
ROMANTIC PLEASURES.

• *Keep in mind that having no love interest in your life at the moment doesn't mean you never will.* Love has a way of surprising us when we least expect it. A person can go years, decades, and suddenly meet a partner. Instead of obsessing on the lack of a love object, deepen your friendships and engage your interests more intensely. If you take this opportunity to make your life fuller, you'll have more to bring to a relationship if or when one comes along.

• *Don't compare your single status unfavorably to the marriages of others.* Remember that being coupled guarantees neither a satisfying sexual relationship nor a pleasant companionship. (Check out the divorce statistics.) Concentrate on the loving connections you have in your life, not on what is missing, and remember that if you want a relationship and are willing to really work at having one, chances are you can achieve it.

• *Remember that you won't die of a lack of erotic love in your life.* It is something to be desired but it doesn't damage your physical or mental health to be without it for even extended periods of time. Many have lived quite fulfilled lives and have often achieved greatness by sublimating their sexual desire into other pursuits.

• *Think outside conventional notions of romance and include friendships with the opposite sex.* Be aware that romance has more possibilities than sexual consummation. Unconscious sexual desire can be sublimated into deep, even passionate, friendships that may in the long run be richer and more stable than a traditional love affair. It's desirable to develop a number of these friendships, each of which brings some special quality (warmth or depth of shared interest) that together will make up for not having a single relationship. Don't pursue friendships that aren't freely given; this will rob you of comfort rather than reward you. Nurture those that will stimulate you and with whom you can be your spontaneous, best self. This group will take time to create but the effort is small compared to the rewards that may endure for a lifetime.

• *Get to know your sexual style.* This will differ depending on your generation, religious background, moral beliefs, personal taste and psychology. For example, can you psychologically handle casual sexual encounters without losing your emotional footing? If not, take care of yourself by only being with those people who can offer the security you're seeking. Are you on a marriage track? If so, mount a campaign (there are mountains of good books around to guide you) and don't flag until you cross the finish line. Or are you interested in an ongoing partner with no live-in strings attached? Analyze your moral, ethical and religious beliefs concerning sex and love and set up guidelines for yourself based on your personal standards and what is best for your happiness.

• *Use living alone—with its protection of friends and personal autonomy—as insurance against being prematurely swept away by romance.* Infatuation is a strong drug and can lead us astray. The more strength and self-respect we have, the less likely that we will overrate a lover (and thereby underrate ourselves), lose our perspective and be vulnerable to an inappropriate romance. Even when we're in love, it's prudent not to neglect our friends of either sex. They are the foundation of our lives and a valuable reality check. The loved one should be a delightful accompaniment to our already intact lives, not the main event.

• *If you are without a love interest for a time, divert erotic energy into creative outlets.* For example, try painting, writing poetry, reading or other deep interests. What Freud called the libido can be sublimated into intense artistic endeavors that have immortalized many artists.

• *Indulge the sensuality of touch.* Join a dance class, enjoy massages, manicures and affectionate exchanges with family and friends.

Your house is your larger body.
It grows in the sun and sleeps in the stillness of
the night; and it is not dreamless.
—KAHLIL GIBRAN

my space my way

(our living space is our closest companion,
always communicating, always reflecting
our process of change)

I have a friend who can't abide any wood showing on the
floor, so reminded is he of the bare boards of his impov-
erished urban childhood during the Depression. He
adores his wall-to-wall carpeting just as I bask in the glow
of polished, unadorned floors and revel in undressed

windows so different from my childhood home in 1950s suburbia.

I can enjoy visiting friends in spaces where choruses of photos serenade from tarnished frames, collectibles shout hosannas from glass cupboards and all manner of memories are immortalized in figurines, dried flowers, framed letters, ribbon-bedecked wedding portraits and other inherited treasures. But one person's symphony is another's cacophony, and though I'm completely charmed by such intimate museums, it would distract me to live in one. These proud curators, on the other hand, feel sensory deprivation in my spare and (to their minds) uncozy digs.

Our surroundings compose a portrait of who we are, what we value and what we think of ourselves. Everything our eyes light upon speaks to us with silent voices, so it's important that they speak kindly. Our home is sifted through the lens of our past; it enters our psyches and infects us with venom or magic. This was most clear to me when I first sampled living on my own. When I was in a relationship, my partner was the primary focus and our home was a stage in which we played out our relationship. We both took an active part in creating it, the atmosphere was "our" taste—molded by compromise—not strictly his or mine and, for the most part, the setting stayed politely in the background. But when my longtime wish to have my own space finally materialized, the background boldly leapt forward and claimed the spotlight. It was cluttered with props—furniture, photographs, crockery, remnants from our past codecoration—that whispered obsolete messages inappropriate to my new life. No longer beholden to a mate, I needed to experiment with my fledgling autonomy and explore my taste, unbridled.

ᕫᕤ

I learned that *my space is my sanctuary, my visual background music, the litmus test of my self-esteem.* The disappearance of ugliness became as satisfying as the presence of beauty; the absence of languishing houseplants and crummy slipcovers, of cracked windows and frayed towels, of closets stuffed with unwearable or unworn clothes. Neglected household objects sketched an unbecoming portrait of my own self-neglect. Lacking a partner to polish my ego, it was up to me to protect myself from sub-liminal messages that were, like daily saboteurs, tarnish-ing my self-esteem.

Anything negative that could build a nest of unworthi-ness in some corner of my psyche had to be banished.

I began to question what I truly liked as opposed to what I was supposed to like. Did I love Grandma's chipped teapot? Yes. It stayed. This distressed towel? Out! How about these grungy mules no one ever sees me wearing? I see me wearing them. Out! They were pro-paganda encouraging me to feel deprived and unworthy of something better. Anything I merely tolerated left the scene, including the Modigliani print that sent me into raptures thirty-five years ago at the Modern; it no longer beguiled. Why should it? I'd changed my taste in read-ing, clothes, food and music. Why be saddled with arti-facts that no longer inspired me?

Unrestrained by a partner, I began to get in touch with my maverick side and unleashed my eccentricities. There was a glorious sense of power in rearranging the furniture at 3 A.M. (putting the bed in the living room with the fireplace), painting a wall apricot on a whim or staying up past dawn, tossing out kitchen cupboard doors to leave the dishes exposed, and then sleeping till noon (actors are mostly unemployed). It was autonomy at its grandest.

Now, for the first time ever, there was no one looking over my shoulder, guiding my decisions, correcting my "mistakes" and teaching me caution. Wings unclipped, there was only me playing with empty space that kneeled to my will. I learned that I prefer old (read drafty), high-ceilinged rooms with moldings, gleaming wood floors, French doors, fireplaces and as few other embellishments as possible. I'm mad for candles and have a distaste for lampshades (which I liken to pesky ballerinas suspended in my airspace), rugs have a floor life of less than a week before being exiled, and if I could do without furniture I would. My friends kindly refrain from giving me little Eiffel Tower pencil sharpeners or the odd cuddly stuffed something for my bed. Though I flee collectibles, I permit books to spawn like reckless moss.

I know from experience that gratifying one's taste isn't necessarily expensive. While traveling through simple Portuguese fishing villages I'd been charmed by white-washed houses with cascading flowers, blue-shuttered windows and a plain wooden table displaying a bowl of fruit. The most satisfying environment I'd ever inhabited was the most inexpensive. It was when my husband and I owned a floundering art gallery and very little else. Financially desperate, we moved into the gallery, one room in an old town house painted white with a white floor. On the walls were abstract paintings lit by pinpoint spotlights. In front of the white marble fireplace we unfolded two canvas chairs, one on each side of a small white table that we'd scavenged from a friend's basement. On it I placed one extravagant rose. Stored in the closet were cushions for sleeping, which also served as seating at dinners that my culinary husband would prepare in a galley kitchen closeted behind white-louvered doors. Firelight, food, monastic simplicity. Heaven. Later, in more elaborate settings, I knew I hadn't improved on that unembellished purity.

As I began to live in my idea of beauty I realized that my surroundings affected me like music. In Portugal I had become almost drunk on the architecture and despaired of finding such visual rapture at home where function so often outweighs form. I wasn't able to move to Europe and live in those singing spaces under fifteenth-century arches, but I hoped I could create, in almost any space, an intimate atmosphere filled with objects that reminded me of beloved others. Every day

barbara feldon

Granddad, his tie blowing in the breeze, smiles across decades from his photo on my desk. In the mornings I eat cereal from a blue and white bowl that my school-mate Janice brought me from France and drink coffee from Grandma's rose-patterned cup. My friend Maxine made me a sculpted wooden horse and it is now a touching sentinel beside the piano that my friend Vito willed to me and that has brought so much music into my life. And every time I gaze into the blue serenity of a Japanese landscape on the willow-patterned platter that belonged to my mother, I feel touched by her presence.

Having my own place has delivered all the heady pleasures I'd imagined since girlhood, plus a striking surprise: *My solitary space was only intermittently solitary.* I was amazed to discover with what freedom the outside world flowed quite naturally through my door and how comfortably it blended with the atmosphere I'd created. A couple of times a week friends relaxed in the candle glow looking like affectionately placed objects; human decor. They arrived and took their leave and arrived again in a rhythm that became reliable and delightful. And after they left, for a while I would leave the candles lit to reflect from the half-empty wine glasses, the roses and silverware and enjoy the leftover resonance of

91

friendship before restoring the rooms to their monastic state.

Our living space is our closest companion, part self, part other relationships, always communicating, always reflecting our process of change.

For me, it has become a diagnostic tool mirroring the condition of my mind; when my home is in disarray chances are so am I. I gain confidence as I *exercise my will* and transform a neutral space into an oasis of autonomy that causes banners of liberation to unfurl in my mind.

Why else is it wondrous to have my own place? Because it is mine. My very own. Not a shade of compromise but purely, deliriously, unconditionally mine. Whether I'm puttering around or reading in my sleeping loft till dawn, my home surrounds me with its endearing presence—filled with familiar creaks and gentle silences—and speaks encouragingly to me as I continue to evolve.

OUR SPACE IS OUR SANCTUARY,
OUR VISUAL BACKGROUND MUSIC,
THE LITMUS TEST OF OUR SELF-ESTEEM.

• *Discover what you like and what you don't like.* This is your chance to be bold. Claim your space: Make it reflect your tolerance for clutter or spareness. If you prize wall-to-wall carpeting go for it, if bare floors are your thing let them shine. Choose wall colors that suit your temperament and slowly add only those furnishings that appeal to you. Scan magazines and notice what kind of decor (or lack of it) catches your fancy. Sort through your possessions—photos, artwork, knickknacks, crockery—and choose the objects that please you, then diligently give away or discard the rest. It's better to live with a few things than with those that don't express your taste or that deliver outdated, inappropriate or even bitter memories that you should leave behind.

Remember that creating a beautiful atmosphere is not necessarily expensive—what is most beautiful is that which truly represents you.

• *Get rid of (or repair) everything that causes low self-esteem.* Don't underestimate the power of objects. Everyday confrontations by frayed towels or shredding curtains, disabled furniture and peeling paint can represent an unbecoming self-portrait that might erode your self-esteem. Toss out anything that is incurably soiled or so outdated that you will never wear it. Why hang on to anything—pots, dishes, clothes, lamps—that is borderline OK but that you never use? These things create clutter and become dependents that require care and get in your way but give nothing in return. If you have wood floors it's worth the effort to polish them (or for that matter, anything else that has the capacity to shine). Check window frames, ceilings and bathrooms for cracks and take care of them. Creating a "cared for" environment is a way of showing yourself respect and reinforcing it daily.

• *Display objects and photos that remind you of those you love.* Since everything we invite into our environment has a symbolic presence, it's important that we're in friendly territory. The display of an object or a photograph from someone we love reinforces our connection to them. To be reminded of someone who has harmed us in some way poisons the atmosphere we're trying to create and erodes our feeling of well-being. It's better to be rid of them than to have to fight off unpleasant memories.

• *Encourage yourself to be a maverick in your own space.*
If you have an unorthodox desire to sleep on a futon in
a different location in your apartment each night, why
not? If you want to paint the window frames red or
rearrange the furniture every week (something almost
impossible to do with a partner), don't be shy about
doing it. Hang your own paintings if they please you or,
if you're a reader, paste up favorite quotations.

This is your space to do with as you please, a play-
ground where you can create the game with all its
rules without compromise—one of the perks of living
alone.

• *Be aware of your space as you would be of another person.*
It's important, from time to time, to just "be" in it without distractions. Enjoy each of its elements and be sensitive to the little deteriorations that need care. Dress your
space up with fresh flowers if possible and fill it with
music and fragrances you love.

• *Open your door to others.* Remember that it's your
choice to either be solitary or invite the world in. When
you've created an environment that is uniquely yours,
chances are that your friends will be as comfortable

in it as they are with you. Entertaining those we care for leaves memories of friendship and warmth in our home and integrates our solitary space into the larger world.

Erasmus must feed himself and
wear his own feathers.
—Erasmus

money is the root
of autonomy

(financial security is about freedom)

During the forties and fifties, my dad was the money tree that spread protective shade over the household and shed dollars; there was a forest of dads in the community all performing the same service. The idea of a woman being initiated into that mysterious rite was unimaginable; it was a point of pride for men to be the sole support and women to sport the resulting jewelry, washer-dryers and occasional fur piece.

My father, however, broke ranks slightly when I experienced an unexpected brush with fortune at the age of ten. My grandmother, mistakenly believing that she was dying, split her eight shares of General Motors stock (each worth sixty dollars!) between my sister and me; a heady enrichment. Every three months when the quarterly report arrived in the mail, my dad would hand it to me and say gravely, "You'd better review this. You should know what your company is up to." I would stare at the mysterious page, stumped but proud that he seemed to believe I was up to the job. However, this invitation into his economic fraternity conflicted with my plan to wait for a man to prove his love—and consequently my self-worth—by being my financial savior. Foolishly, I chose to ignore my dad's encouragement and instead continued to remain financially ignorant.

All I needed the first few months on my own in New York was a simple policy: scrape together the rent and buy nothing nonessential. Rebelling against my middle-class background, I felt proud of being poor and scoffed at any "bourgeois materialistic" concern for money. When that pose was threatened by winning some hefty cash on a quiz show, I palmed it off onto a young "adviser" through whose fingers it sifted like sand until not a grain was left. I was unfazed—almost relieved, really—and continued sampling the exotic flavor of bohemian poverty, until one hair-raising month when I nearly defaulted on my rent and the phone company demanded a cruelly exorbitant deposit because I was an actress. For the first time I felt the sting of humiliation that is visited upon the penniless and grew nostalgic about my wasted windfall. I took every temp job I could get and tried to save—which was like struggling up a vertical sand dune—but still neglected taking any deeper interest in my money.

Then I married and welcomed the financial shield I'd been awaiting. There were many dear marital rewards in that relationship but I soon realized that financial salvation wasn't one of them. Even so, I harbored a state of denial about my situation because I continued to refuse to take responsibility for my financial security.

❧

A few years into my marriage, it collapsed and I was again on my own. When my career experienced an uptick and I enjoyed a modest surplus in the bank, I immediately groped for an investment guru. He appeared in the guise of a twenty-something fast-track broker trading stocks he referred to as "sexy," which meant they bounced around like a bungee jumper. The economy was hot, expense accounts were bountiful, everyone was optimistic, which, unbeknownst to me, spelled disaster. I was Little Red Riding Hood skipping through the forest on her way to the wolf when, luckily, I was headed off by my first financial mentor.

Ralph wasn't a materialist but, as a survivor of the Depression, he took money seriously. He was alarmed by my hands-off policy regarding my finances.

"Don't you think you ought to pay attention to your money?" he asked.

I showed disdain, arguing that our materialistic culture tended to find meaning in "things." We agreed that material things rarely brought happiness; in fact, their "magic" evaporates swiftly.

Then he said, "But *caring for money is not about being able to buy things, it's about freedom.* Its real value is insurance against crippling anxiety if your career falters. How can you have a fulfilling life (and isn't that *vital*?) if you're crushed by debt and insecurity?"

I admitted that this was a refreshing way to look at it; even so, lethargy claimed me at the hint of having to balance my checkbook. When I tried to suppress a yawn Ralph noted it and grinned.

"It may feel tedious, but that isn't the only reason you resist controlling your money. You just don't want to give up the idea of having someone who will take care of the problem for you. It's a hard fantasy to sacrifice."

I must have looked offended by his blunt assessment because he tried to mollify me. "It's not only women who resist controlling their money. Many very successful men are financially undone by a childlike wish to be taken care of, too. How do you think credit card companies became so successful? They play the indulgent parent and tempt people into debt from which many never recover."

I didn't need to be warned of the results of not paying off my credit card each month, having observed the struggle of a friend who has become a slave to credit card interest. To date she has paid double the original debt in interest with no hope of ending her bondage.

Over the next few months, whenever Ralph and I met for coffee, he prodded me like a devil with a pitchfork to rescue my imperiled finances.

"So your policy is to hand over your money to a so-called 'financial expert' and then knock on wood," he shook his head. "You're putting your entire financial future at risk. Don't you think you should begin educating yourself about economics?"

He wrote something on a paper napkin and handed it to me. It was a list of financial periodicals and books on economics and investing.

"Are you serious?" I laughed. "I'm the kid who never turned in a homework assignment! And, anyway, who am I to presume to handle my own investments?"

"Who are you *not* to?" he countered. "*It's your money.* You're living on your own and you're in a cliff-hanging business that is famously unkind to women. Who's going to protect you? Do you want to abandon your money to just anybody and risk ending up with nothing? Or are you willing to become your own benefactor?"

Visions of being a bag lady hunched on a curb, my feet wrapped in burlap, spurred me to hastily withdraw my funds from the hands of my frisky broker, flee the overheated stock market and begin drilling my way through a mountain of financial books and periodicals. (Two years later the market collapsed and, though I had succumbed to many a doze during my studies, I observed that not one expert had predicted it.)

But this was only basic training. Ralph then nudged

me up to the front lines where, after reading through wildly varying investment advice, he expected me to take action. When I complained of confusion, he quoted, "When in doubt, do nothing," and sent me in search of more clarity by harvesting the thoughts of people with special expertise—a banker, an investment counselor, a friend who was an economist—and then comparing their opinions. When I flagged and seemed about to dump the problem into a single expert's lap he warned me, *"Make your own mistakes, not somebody else's."*

Armed with that invaluable advice I tremulously started to make investment decisions, and though I may have erred on the side of a too conservative portfolio, I've managed over the years to sleep peacefully through both bull and bear markets.

$\backsim$

Ralph's program for me became more exhaustive, a kind of commando training for financial combat. He urged me to become intimately involved with every facet of my money. Every expense must be ferreted out and factored in: traffic tickets, postage stamps, gifts, movies, taxis, contributions, tax preparation, even fugitive expenses like the spontaneous treats I used as mood elevators: manicures, the odd lingerie addition. I argued that this wasn't really necessary for me to do because my policy was to buy only essentials and save everything else.

"Which is why," I announced proudly, "I have excess funds to invest."

"But that's as unbalanced as spending lavishly," he laughed. "It's just another way of not dealing with money. The point isn't to just save mindlessly and end up a dead old lady in a homeless shelter with a million dollars strapped to your waist. You don't need a lot of money, just enough to live comfortably and be free from anxiety; beyond that it's just a pile of green stuff without meaning. Your purpose should be to understand how much you have, figure out your expenses, save a reasonable amount for the future and *enjoy* the rest. There are other essentials for your happiness, you know: concerts, traveling, entertaining, books."

I emerged from this exercise with a more realistic grasp of my situation. But there were still more discomforts to face: the doomy prospect of my will, for example, and the anxiety-producing puzzlements of insurance. I wanted to escape into a novel, see a movie, go to sleep, anything but study a confusing prospectus or the small print of my mortgage contract. Ralph diligently prodded me forward until I had achieved a fair grasp of the overall financial picture and had some assurance that I could weather the tides of my profession.

Now one would think that I'd welcome this mastery, but instead I felt a sullen sense of loss (despite my feminist beliefs). By giving up my pose of damsel in distress, I had erased the prospect of rescue by a knight in shining armor (a significant letdown for a romantic). Independence seemed a drabber thrill than being dependent and was a lot more trouble. Every financial issue I solved, everything I bought for myself was in conflict with childhood wishes to be taken care of.

Over time, in spite of myself, I began to relish my increasing control over my money and grudgingly accepted the role of caretaker. Then finally I enjoyed the inner security and self-esteem I'd gained from commandeering my finances and felt deeply indebted to my generous mentor for guiding me toward financial autonomy. I had become the money tree spreading protective shade over my own life without which I could never have explored the pleasures of living alone with such a light heart and easy mind.

WE ARE OUR OWN BENEFACTORS.

• *Examine your attitude about money.* What does it mean to you? Have you resisted taking charge of your finances? If so, try and understand why. If you have lingering dreams of being taken care of, notice the pitfalls of that fantasy as opposed to the advantages of becoming your own benefactor. Remember, it's difficult to have a good time living alone if you feel vulnerable and financially threatened.

• *In a notebook or a computer program like Quicken list every topic pertaining to your financial life and systematically focus on each issue.* You can list topics like bank accounts, IRAs, investments, will, mortgage or lease and insurance policies. Under each heading note all the actions you need to take regarding each factor. This can feel overwhelming at first so don't force yourself to solve everything at once. The important thing is to list meticulously what you have to attend to. As you become accustomed to taking control you will, little by little, work your way through to mastery over every element. Update the notebook every month (perhaps when you get your bank statement) and make any adjustments that are necessary.

• *Fearlessly list every one of your expenses.* This can include wardrobe, car, rent, household, insurance and medical expenses. Include Christmas and birthday gifts, wedding presents, impulse purchases, tips for deliveries, the paper you bought because you forgot what time the movie started. Since socializing is important to the enjoyment of living alone, factor in restaurants, entertaining expenses and even the wardrobe you might need. List expenses for things that contribute to your growth and happiness: concerts, museums, classes, hobbies.

• *Living within your means is simple arithmetic.* Compute your income from your job and investments then compare it to your expenses. If your income doesn't cover your expenses *with a residue for unforeseen emergencies,* ruthlessly cut back on expenditures or consider subsidiary work. Remember that owning things doesn't bring happiness, but living within the bounds of your income can—no matter how modest. It is *essential* for your sense of security and peace of mind.

• *Never use a credit card unless you can pay it off monthly.* There is no advantage to long-term credit card debt. Credit card companies prey on our desire to have a Big

Daddy who will take care of us and provide immediate gratification. It's in their interest to coax us into debt so they can collect exorbitant interest rates. Incurring interest debt is a classic way to sink yourself financially and rob you, perhaps for years or forever, of the autonomy so essential to enjoying living on your own.

• *Gradually invest for the future.* If you start early enough, your investments will grow to a sturdy amount in just a few decades. Get to know the economic style most comfortable for you; some people can relax with the stock market, it gives others the willies and they will sleep more easily by clipping coupons. If you're shaky about a financial decision, gather several other opinions on which to base *your own judgment*. You might find this information in books and periodicals, from an acquaintance or from meetings with experts. Be wary of euphoric trends that can end disastrously. Read the financial page in your paper to get an overview of the economy; it could be helpful in anticipating trends that might affect you. Your future is in your hands; you want to protect it like a caring parent.

• *Open an IRA to shelter some of your income.* This is a fine way to build a nest egg for the future.

• *Review every one of your insurance policies to be sure you are adequately covered.* Make sure you have health insurance, personal liability insurance, car coverage, and if you are past middle age, consider long-term health-care insurance. Once you have the insurance in place, review it periodically to see if it needs updating.

• *Make a will.* Just bite the bullet and get it over with.

• *Give up the idea of there being an ideal caretaker who will provide a safe haven and relieve you of responsibility for your financial security.* *You* are your safest haven if you're willing to take charge of *every aspect* of your economic life, no matter how tedious or overwhelming it might seem at first. The ultimate goal isn't acquiring a fortune, it's to be free from concern in order to enjoy the adventure of living alone.

Don't look outside yourself for a leader.
—*H*OPI ELDERS AFTER THE
*S*EPTEMBER 11, 2001, *TERROR ATTACKS*

alone in a time of crisis

(there are many dangers to be concerned about in a crisis; living alone is not one of them)

I sleep in a small atticlike room perched above a garden that stretches peacefully through the interior of my noisy city block. My bed is littered with books that I indulgently read until near dawn; the skylight gazes down like a benevolent eye. I have never felt lonely in this nesting space until the night after the World Trade Center attack.

Along with the rest of the country on September 11, 2001, I spent the day in uncomprehending horror as, again and again, we watched the towers crash and melt over a pitiful chaos of humanity. Shaken friends phoned reaching out for comfort and for the anchor of each other, but there was no comfort and no one could imagine feeling anchored again. Oddly, though we often shared meals, we didn't make plans to get together. Rather, we seemed to need solitude to process the day's ghastly events.

To avoid nightmares, I clung to the TV coverage that stretched mercifully into the night. About four-thirty in the morning I climbed the narrow staircase to my loft and lay down alone—as alone as I can ever remember feeling. I questioned my single lifestyle and ached for the consolation of a body next to mine; a man to hold me, soften my grief and make me feel safe. In retrospect I realize what I really wanted in the guise of a partner was my mother. Not the mother whom I got to know as an adult, but the original *Mommy* with the power to banish the terror of a five-year-old.

When I was a child we lived next to a woods on a solitary hill. At night I imagined a wolf was creeping from its lair, climbing the side of the house and about to lunge through my bedroom window. Since my father was a traveling businessman and rarely home, my sole defense against wolves was Mother, five feet, four inches of absolute security. It was she to whom I ran in the middle of the night—when lightning threatened to stab through my window and thunder crashed over me like a falling building—to restore my sense of safety. (I now know that after reassuring me, Mother would lie awake, cold with fear, as she imagined a murderer creeping from the woods toward the house. She checked the bedside table for the gun and longed for Father to be home holding her, soothing her fear as *her* mother had.)

But married friends have since told me there was scant comfort in companionship the night of 9/11. My friend Ellen said, "Even with my husband I was frightened. Contemplating one's mortality is a solitary adventure." Whether a loved one was lying beside us or not, that night we each lay in bed bereft and scared; there were no "mommies" to chase away the wolves.

ح

The following days, though I stayed alone I felt a comforting connection to others. Even commentators and public figures reached through our TV screens and pulled together a wounded community, shared our grief and tried to make the hideous reality comprehensible. As individual tragedies unfolded we wept together with the families of the victims; a tribe mourning a catastrophe of mythic proportions. We were not isolated individuals, we became a people.

Another kind of consolation blossomed as e-mails flew among friends creating a chain reaction of forwarded stories that drew us into the hearts of the victims and rescue workers. On the street, as the smoke began to subside, a shroud of ashes seemed to settle over the collective psyche of the city, the usual bustle and fizz replaced by a solemn mood we all shared. It seemed natural to speak to strangers as if our human iron curtains had crumpled along with the buildings, as though we knew one another intimately. And in our shared grief and vulnerability, we did. I never felt safer on the streets—and I never felt less alone.

After the first shock subsided a second wave united us: the grief that our country—as New Yorkers, our city—had been horribly violated. One evening at twilight I walked through Central Park and stood looking south across the green swath of Sheep Meadow to the skyline of Central Park South. In the pearl light the tops of buildings shone like a miniature Acropolis; this was the city where I had dreamed of living since I was a ten-year-old admiring its thrilling portraits in *Life* magazine. Most residents feel a love-hate relationship with New York; that evening there was no hate, only a love as romantically engaging as that for an individual.

Then a third wave crashed down upon us. Fear. What might come next? When and in what form? Can we protect ourselves? How? Who has the answers? Do any answers exist?

When I first began to live alone I feared having to face such a crisis solo. I believed that I would need to be with someone on whom my very life might depend. I've since learned that such dependency can be dangerous unless the person on whom I'm leaning happens to be an expert on how to deal with the situation at hand.

❧

After the 9/11 attack the fear of death afflicted each of us according to our temperaments and there was no immediate reassurance. I remembered once hearing a radio interview with Bertrand Russell on his ninety-sixth birthday. He was asked how he felt about the future in view of his advanced age. He answered, "The same as I've always felt about everything: *We must act with vigor in the face of uncertainty.*" It was necessary now to act with vigor, become my own reconnaissance operation, piece together information like bits of a jigsaw puzzle, analyze the picture and decide what to do. This did not require a partner, but neither could it be accomplished alone. It needed TV and radio information, and the helping hands of the Internet and anyone I knew who could provide constructive advice. Within a few days a chorus of sources addressed survival necessities and escape routes, and enough relief organizations were identified to suit any temperament or neuroses; no one living alone could complain of being bereft of help.

$\mathcal{C}$

The Greeks said, "Know thyself," which is perhaps not entirely possible. But a crisis is a great opportunity to shake hands with dormant aspects of ourselves. The 9/11 attack reintroduced me to one of my quiescent phobias:

germs. Before retiring one Friday night I checked the TV for breaking news and received warnings of an attack expected during the coming weekend. This was unnerving, but I remembered my friend Ralph saying, "When in doubt, do nothing," whenever I was facing my own confusion, and so I settled in for the evening. Then came the government's concerns that the attack would be chemical or biological. My doubt evaporated. I knew exactly what I wanted to do: I wanted to be somewhere else! I squelched my embarrassment at behaving like a wimp; a bomb I could handle, but I really, *really* wasn't up for germs!

When I was six years old I developed a contamination phobia and became a one-kid FBI, shunning door knobs and driving my parents nuts by compulsively investigating every molecule of food on my plate. (What did I imagine was lurking in the lettuce?) I eventually outgrew those fears, but extreme stress can temporarily knock me back into childhood where they reside. Instead of toughing them out, I've learned to take pity on my beleaguered psyche and do whatever is within my power to make life as anxiety-free as possible no matter how silly my actions may appear to others.

When you're living alone, there is no one to second

guess your decisions, no one campaigning to make you think rationally when fear has broken through the Maginot line of reason. Of course, there is no one to shed light on your reactions, either, so you learn to monitor your own state of mind and seek ways to comfort yourself.

Feeling threatened and not relishing insomnia, I called a New Jersey friend and asked if he was planning to be in Manhattan that evening. He was. Would he mind dropping me at a motel in New Jersey on his way home? (I planned to take books to entertain myself in that microbe-free haven.) John generously drove me to his family's house at the Jersey shore where I spent an unrattled weekend, and Monday I returned to a blessedly uncontaminated New York with my composure restored. I was honoring my vulnerabilities until I could collect information that would prevent me from either exaggerating dangers or denying them.

How imperiled are we? Is New York a target? Is the water supply endangered? What about gas masks—a good idea or irrelevant? How dangerous are the subways? How safe are airplanes? Although the media spared us no fearsome detail, paradoxically, *the more I learned the less anxious I felt.* Here were real dangers and it was a relief to face them. I began assessing each issue one by one; if I took no action it would at least be *my* decision. If I needed to be saved, I would have to save myself.

❧

I soon became aware of my appalling lack of knowledge; in school we barely acknowledged Europe, much less the Middle East. I had a trace memory of the name Ottoman Empire, but beyond that my Middle Eastern education didn't extend beyond seeing Peter O'Toole play Lawrence of Arabia. Looking at maps I was jolted to see places I'd never heard of: Turjikstan. Islamabad. How did Iran get directly west of Afghanistan? I slunk to the bookstore and joined other embarrassed New Yorkers crowding in front of the histories of Islam and the Mideast. (Even in my ignorance I wasn't alone!) In the weeks of reading that followed I acquired not only a greater understanding of the current situation, but a thirst to know more about the region, its history, art and literature. There are collateral benefits to taking action.

I've polled my single friends to hear their reaction to being alone during the attack. My friend Sara immediately rushed to the Red Cross to help out. Since they were swamped with volunteers she went home and baked cookies to deliver to the rescue teams. "I had no perception of being alone," she said. "I immediately found comfort in the rescue effort." Ann went to donate blood, Carol spent time with others at a Buddhist temple in her neighborhood and Tony helped out at Saint Patrick's Cathedral.

There are many things to be concerned about in a crisis; living alone is certainly not one of them. It's a time to unite with others, to work together, mourn together, an opportunity to learn that once you accept responsibility for your well-being you can become your own best protector.

BECOME YOUR OWN BEST PROTECTOR
IN A TIME OF CRISIS.

• *Connect with others.* Reach out to friends to share reactions and anxieties and for mutual comfort. If you live in an apartment building, check in with neighbors; when on the street, be open to exchanging your impressions with others. Be aware that you are not alone but part of a community that is sharing your distress. Go to a place where you can help out.

• *Get involved with the community.* Action is bracing; volunteer your services. Being involved with others in a common effort is rewarding for the community, but especially for yourself. Check out your local church, temple, mosque, Red Cross, Salvation Army or other charitable organizations to see how you might help. Contribute food, clothing and money where you feel it will be the most helpful. Attend services and public forums where you can offer your views and share your concerns with others.

• *Gather facts.* Watch coverage on TV and listen to the radio for information and news as it unfolds. Study newspapers for in-depth insights and seek specialized information on the Internet. If you know anyone with expertise, contact them to help deepen your knowledge. Ignorance breeds anxiety, information puts you more in control. Each piece of the puzzle will broaden the picture and contribute to your plan of action.

• *Take charge of your own destiny.* There is no absolute outside authority. Don't depend solely on a loved one or friend for solutions; a close relationship provides many wonderful things, but saving your life isn't one of them. Based on reliable information take steps to protect yourself both physically and psychologically. Make a list of emergency needs and procedures: escape routes, emergency phone numbers, food and water supplies, transistor radio, medications. Keep a kit of these provisions at hand. Planning in advance can reduce confusion and help you avoid panic in case an emergency arises. If you never need them, so much the better.

• *Honor your fragilities.* Be kind to yourself and don't be embarrassed by your personal aversions; we each have a unique array of fears. In a time of insecurity don't increase your anxiety by forcing yourself to take brave actions you are uncomfortable with. Remember, those who appear to be braver than we, may be foolhardy or simply not scared. If you want to avoid flying, do so. If a cupboard full of bottled water comforts you, stock up. If owning a gas mask will help you sleep better, buy one. If you want to vacate the area for a while, arrange to leave.

• *Use the flood of information during a crisis to broaden your interest in the issues and people involved.* In addition to newspaper, magazine and Internet articles, peruse books in the library and bookstores. This is an opportunity to understand the causes of disasters and to become familiar with people, places, religion and politics in a way that will enrich your world and challenge you intellectually.

• *Apply these principles to any situation you regard as a crisis.* Whether it's a medical emergency or any threat to yourself or others, gather information from a variety of sources and do what is necessary to protect yourself physically and emotionally.

It is not so much our friends' help that helps us
but the certain knowledge that they will help us.
—EPICURUS

braving it together: goal groups

(the point is sharing)

So here we are, examining all the little shards of our lives, trying to piece them together into a satisfying picture, and doing it all by ourselves. It's confusing, it's hard, it's dreary, it's lonely. Living alone is a challenge and requires focus. We need to set priorities and pursue goals, but isn't there a better way than soldiering on alone?

There is: Form a goal group. *Goal groups work.* I'm not sure how, they just do; maybe because we're herd animals, happy with our fellows but tending to wilt in isolation. Maybe stating our aims clarifies them for us and a tribal gene makes us accountable to our team effort.

"I couldn't get it together after my divorce," Marie said. "I was out there by myself, my social life smashed along with the marriage. I hadn't the energy to begin shaping a new life. I felt orphaned. No structure, no ideas. Then a friend, Casey Kelly, told me about a goal setter's group she was creating of ten men and women who were discontented with where they were in their lives and wanted to make changes. She invited me to meet with them once every six weeks to set goals and discuss our progress. When I arrived, I felt uneasy about airing my personal situation in front of a group of strangers, but I soon joined the others and began defining my goals. First we wrote down all the things we wanted to do, be or have, then starred and double-starred them in order of importance.

"Since I live alone, building a social life was my primary goal. Beyond that I wanted to get more involved with art. I remember the pleasure, when I was a teenager, of watercolor painting. I used to go to restaurants armed with a miniature paint set so I could do quick sketches of the patrons. I found those sketchbooks recently and felt regret that this interest had gotten buried under the time pressures of work and marriage.

"Each of us stated our goals and the obstacles to them (in my case shyness), then planned ways to overcome the obstacles before the next meeting. Being in the presence of others inspired me to think of actions I hadn't conceived of on my own. First, I decided to join a gym because I needed structure in my life that wasn't isolated. I also needed to make friends, so I identified two people at my workplace whom I might invite to lunch. One of the members suggested I think of ways to incorporate art into my social goals: Bring a friend to the museum or other art exhibitions, or look for a group that arranges outings to paint landscapes.

"Now, the strange thing is, I rarely thought about the group during the weeks that followed but I must have felt a solidarity with them that motivated me because when we met again I was amazed at my progress. I'd been working out at a gym, I'd had lunch with a colleague and I'd contacted a local university to get information about their extension art classes.

"Well, that was three years ago and now I have a number of great friends, have completed several terrific painting classes at the university where I've met more friends, and host Saturday afternoon painting sessions at my home. I know I wouldn't have done this on my own. *The goal group gave me a braver, more dedicated persona that I internalized.* It wasn't necessary to socialize with members because *the group itself transcends individuals; it inspires more diligence and provides more support than any single member can.*"

I belong to Marie's goal group. Every sixth Sunday we meet at my apartment. Everyone contributes snacks, we chat briefly, then begin. For ten minutes (we use a timer although we're not militant about the time allotted and often allow a member to speak longer if there's a crucial issue at stake) we each review our long- and short-term goals and relate our progress. The group then gives five minutes of supportive thoughts and suggestions—never negative criticism, this isn't goal jail! At one meeting, Casey, our founder, had to decide whether to move to Houston to achieve her solvency goal or to tough it out in her beloved New York. We took extra time to understand her dilemma and then supported her decision to pursue her goal in spite of our mutual loss.

Our group required a commitment of three years. At first I was resistant to pledging myself to such a long period of time, especially to strangers; I felt I could achieve my goals on my own, thank you. But the fact was I hadn't. Nor had anyone else. Gary, a writer, had spent years in Los Angeles writing sitcoms. His goal was to make a living in New York City (an infertile field for comedy writers). During the first few sessions he lamented his inability to overcome the dearth of opportunities here and feared having to retreat to California. Then he started to think less conventionally. His report began to be peppered with enthusiasm for a Web site he'd created called Stupid.com where he could exercise his talent by writing jokes and funny stories, creating games and selling silly kinds of candy. At first only a few people a week visited his site, then hundreds came, then thousands. Two years later Gary turned down a million-dollar offer for his site in order to continue the fun of his now lucrative business.

My goal was to create a living space that was organized, repaired and aesthetically delighting to me. I had the habit of "making do" with windows that didn't close, closets that were out of control and unruly business papers. My nonfunctioning oven, for years a repository for unanswered fan mail, reminded me of my desk in grade school that was so overwhelmed with disorganized papers that the lid couldn't close. I clung to furniture that was ready for a yard sale and to a weary palm plant that was beyond resuscitation. Over the next three years I wrestled with each element (and myself) and finally, defeated by my lack of design skills, I solved the obstacle by soliciting my gifted friend Marilyn Glass. I now live in what is, for me, a wonderful environment; one that has freed me to focus on my next goals: singing and writing.

⟡

It's stunning how effective the process is in spite of very little conscious thought about the group between sessions. In part, this is due to the character of the participants. *Goal members are all highly motivated to change and so they become role models for one another.* As our team members devote themselves to their goals we are inspired to follow suit. As we all know, change is not easy to embrace. A therapist once told me, "The last thing my patients want is to change. They come for relief from pain and change happens in spite of them."

Our group originally had twelve members; nine remain. One middle-aged woman's goal was to overcome her inhibition about meeting men, get married and have a child. After three years she met, married and rode into the sunset with her husband and, at fifty, gave birth to a beautiful girl! Another left once he had achieved his goal of making his business profitable, satisfied that there was nothing further he wished to work on.

Though the rest of us have successfully accomplished our primary goals, we've been unwilling to dismantle our tribe and instead have tackled secondary goals. We would have missed the support and goodwill of our clan in a setting that is different from a relationship. The high stakes of marriage with its built-in vulnerabilities are neutralized in this less intense format. The guidelines of the group— simple support and noninterference—protect members from the complications that can ensue from even the most well-intentioned partner.

Although the members of our group have a variety of goals, a group can also be organized around a theme; living alone, for example. Members might go at their own pace to overcome the obstacles blocking their enjoyment of living on their own, or you could set the agenda for each meeting to focus on social life, finances, loneliness. You can also form a one-on-one goal partnership to develop specific pursuits. I share my writing with a playwright once a week. We order take-out Thai food (with extra peanut sauce), then he reads and talks about his project, after which I read and discuss my own. We've each produced more writing in one year (this book, for example!) than we had in the previous five years combined. We attribute our success to having consistent support and faith in each other's devotion to reaching our goals. After dessert we put aside our own writing and spend the rest of the evening reading aloud passages from our favorite books. Beautiful!

Involving others in our goals doesn't just double our strength, it seems to quadruple it! The point is sharing. Sharing our journeys with all their hardships and setbacks, triumphs and pleasures helps us blossom and proves that we never need to face our challenges completely alone.

barbara feldon

THE GOAL GROUP TRANSCENDS ANY ONE INDIVIDUAL
AND INSPIRES MORE DILIGENCE AND PROVIDES MORE
SUPPORT THAN ANY SINGLE MEMBER CAN.

• *Take the initiative to form a goal group.* Members might
be selected from among friends or friends of friends but
restrict it only to those whom you judge to be highly
motivated to achieve their goals. You might float the idea
to your church group or other organizations with which
you have connections. It isn't essential that you know the
participants: What bonds the group isn't necessarily
social compatibility or common interests, it's your united
effort to change. Once the group is established avoid
opening it to additional members (unless your ranks are
depleted); there's an ecology of intimacy that you won't
want to disturb.

• *Select only sympathetic and highly motivated members.*
The success of the group depends on goodwill, support,
noninterference and each participant's determination to
be diligent in the pursuit of his or her goals. To create an
atmosphere of acceptance, it's important that members
listen intently, respond generously and be understanding
and nonjudgmental. There should be tolerance for what-

131

ever time it takes for a member to progress; no one's getting graded. Each member might contribute some light refreshments: juice, coffee, cookies or other snacks.

• *When you form a goal group each member should establish personal goals such as working through living-alone difficulties or accomplishing specific projects.* Pledge to gather regularly for a set period of time, say three years if the meetings are widely spaced (you'll be amazed at how quickly time evaporates) or for a shorter period if you're meeting every week.

• *To find your personal goal make a list of everything you wish to do, be or have, then star and double-star choices that are still possible in order of their importance to you.* Identify your short- and long-term goals based on what will contribute to your happiness. If the group is dealing solely with living alone, either let each member work through personal issues at his or her own speed or choose a topic for each session, such as loneliness, social integration or financial well-being.

• *Limit the number of minutes each member can speak using a timer.* It's more sensitive than assigning someone the duty of interrupting. Ten minutes should be adequate if the group is large; with fewer participants you may want to allow more time. The group response could be five minutes or more depending on the group size. Sometimes it's important to allow more time if a member has a pressing issue to work through.

• *There is no time limit for success.* At each meeting the members should begin by reiterating their goal, then proceed to report their progress since the last meeting. If there has been little accomplished it's helpful for the person to describe the obstacles that have inhibited going forward and suggest ways of overcoming them.

• *It's fine to change a goal.* Sometimes in the pursuit of a goal it becomes clear that there is a more enriching path to take. The member should explain the new direction so the group understands that the change isn't destructive or merely an evasion of the earlier goal.

• *When members wish to leave the group let them go without pressure.* Going forward and making changes (even for the better) can feel threatening and we have to be ready for it; not everyone is. Being supportive of the departing member's autonomy will leave the door open for him or her to reenter sometime in the future if he or she decides to choose a goal again. Those who have achieved their goals and wish to move on are to be celebrated; it's a tribute to the effectiveness of the group that they are leaving.

From this hour I ordain myself loos'd
of limits and imaginary lines,
Going where I list, my own master
total and absolute . . .
—WALT WHITMAN

traveling solo

(a stranger is not an alien—
we all have something to share)

I'd always marveled at those stories of Victorian women trekking alone through the Sahara or camping out in the frigid wilderness of Tibet. How glorious, I thought, to brave the world on one's own without a man to run offense or, for that matter, without a companion of either sex. I imagined the chest-thumping mastery of every difficulty, the liberty of wafting where I chose without battling a partner's resistance; free to be changed by the whimsy of chance, free to be me—a thrilling Mistress of the Universe. This fantasy was as romantic to me as a movie shot in soft focus.

Yet, now that I'd been living on my own for a few months and had no traveling partner, I hesitated. What about the "being alone" part? With whom could I share impressions: the sunsets, the strange food, the amusing bathroom facilities? To whom could I turn to point out a vine-draped hillside in Italy or discuss the flirting couple at the next table? With whom could I stand on the terrace of a villa admiring lemon trees glowing in the Riviera moonlight? What about the horrible glitches, broken car axles, misunderstood directions, hostile natives?

Although I had traveled for work I was always met at the airport and immediately embraced into the company that had hired me. I had never traveled alone. Never. Judiciously, I postponed a solo trip abroad and decided to try my hand at a more tepid adventure, the California coast. It would feel liberating to take detours and see sites that in the past had bored my partner; conversely, I could happily pass up tourist attractions that would have fascinated him but didn't appeal to me. Although I set out with the expectation of feeling isolated, I was shocked to discover that, without a companion, I seldom felt alone.

∾

When I was coupled, I'd been part of a fortress of two; entrenched, formidable. Alone I was vulnerable and approachable. Whenever I stopped for coffee or to admire a view of the ocean, usually there were others doing the same thing. A couple from Japan handed me a camera and asked me to photograph them with the ocean in the background. They were eager to practice their English and together we laughed while trying to decode each other's meaning. A young woman with a backpack was leaning on the parapet scanning the water for sea lions and I asked if she would like to use my binoculars. We shared them for a few minutes in a futile effort to spy anything fishlike; but we smiled warmly at each other and when we finally gave up and parted ways I returned to my car appreciating the encounter. I realized, for the first time, that *a stranger is not an alien; we all have something in common.* Every encounter fortified my impression of the world as being a far more welcoming place than I had imagined. Yes, the axle did break but several people stopped to help me. In fact, the mechanic took me to his mother's house to spend the night!

But, actually, how tough a challenge was it? After all, I speak the language and I'm often recognized as Secret Agent "99." The real test would come when I traveled alone in a foreign country, one not as saturated with television. I'd always wanted to visit the Incan ruins at Machu Picchu so I flew to Peru. It was not the same. It was even better. When I left the small plane that brought us from Lima to Cuzco (the jump-off to Machu Picchu) I entered an ancient world. Since the altitude caused my heart to sprint, I gratefully surrendered my bag to a sympathetic guide who carried it to the hotel and settled me in my room with a cup of coca tea to ease me into being thirteen thousand feet up in the Andes.

Not only did my altitude-racked body feel unreal, everywhere I looked that night as I walked the streets of this preserved city had a dreamlike quality. The peasant women in top hats and colorful flared skirts weren't costumed for tourists—this was how they still dressed, like characters in a storybook. I felt like a reader who had accidentally stepped into its pages and was wandering around quite happily out of place. All connection I had with the reality of my life back home, with its teeming activities and friends, dissolved in the novelty of this parallel realm that enveloped me so completely that I had no sense of being alone. For the next week an Incan-flavored world replaced my old one, with the advantage that, because I was a visitor, I was excused from any obligation to construct a real life out of its magical elements. And because I was alone I was unencumbered with any reminders of home—even a companion—and undistracted by anyone else's taste, timetable or impressions. I was free to randomly absorb the surprises of children's antics or transactions at the market and, at night, undeterred from roaming alone through an old area of mud huts on streets looped with wires culminating every so often in a sixty-watt bulb.

If I had not been alone I wouldn't have hired a guide to accompany me to Machu Picchu and would have missed a valuable conversation with him. On the train he said, "I'll never leave Cuzco."

"Why not?" I asked.

"I have friends who have moved to Lima or the United States and they have many things I don't have— TV and cars—but they've become more and more alienated. Here I'm surrounded by three generations of my family. Every day when I walk down the street, friends smile and wave or stop to talk." Then he put his hand on his chest and said, "Here in Cuzco, my heart is happy."

This wisdom brought tears to my eyes. I knew few people back home who could make that statement. And if I hadn't been alone I wouldn't have been invited, at Machu Picchu, to join a couple for dinner with whom I became friends. And, in my room (devoid of electricity) I had to be alone in the jet dark to sense the sinister mysteries of Machu Picchu outside my window, and to feel a personal redemption as the dawn spread its comforting light across the ruins in the morning.

Absorbed in the people I met, the architecture and the natural splendor of Peru, at no time did I experience loneliness, only regret when the trip was over. *There can be no loneliness when there is a connection with the culture, the people and the place itself.*

❧

At its best, traveling alone is a joy; at its worst it is instructive. A few months after I'd left my relationship, I remember languishing in New York's cement-melting heat with no work and no friends in town. It was August and desolation was gaining on me. I needed to escape. I remembered once feeling very cheerful on the Riviera so I impulsively packed off to Nice. I arrived at the height of the season and with grave difficulty, found a room in a tacky, summer-exhausted hotel where the surly bell hop dumped my luggage in a "chambre" that looked defeated by the hoards of tourists who had molested it. At dinner in a neon-lighted restaurant I sat wrapped in my gloom and didn't make eye contact with anyone except my militant waiter. That night, in the sallow light of my cell, loneliness, the personal virus I had brought from New York, engulfed me.

By morning I felt not only dreary but alarmed. I remembered once driving with my husband over the Pyrenees, clinging to the door handle as I peered down into a three-thousand-foot gorge. Bowing to my fear of heights I canceled my car, flew to Paris and rented a Peugeot with the intention of driving through wine country. But hotel after hotel turned me away and I despaired of finding a room. As I lunched in a bistro I supplemented my loneliness by wistfully eyeing families chatting among themselves, cozy in their Frenchness while I was drooping on the wrong side of the language barrier. Dreading another sleepless night I raced for Calais on the coast, boarded a boat for England, threw myself on the mercy of a friend for a couple of days, then retreated to New York drearier than ever.

e⌒

What had I done wrong?

Everything. In a desperate attempt to escape loneliness I'd flung myself into a foreign country at the height of the tourist season without reservations and with the guarantee of feeling further isolated by being unable to speak the language. It might have worked if everything had gone right but it didn't, and, being depressed, I was at my least resourceful and unable to find my predicament amusing. Since I was viewing the world through the lens of loneliness I was also less inclined to connect with others, the very remedy that would have made a difference. It would have been far better to travel with a group, take a cruise, travel from a passionate desire to experience a new place: its people, architecture, art or historical sites. Then I would have enthusiastically embraced whatever or whomever I encountered. But my motivation was a negative one. I was trying to escape a mood but it never left my side. I didn't connect with Nice, with the French or with other tourists; I was bolted into the distressing loneliness I had attempted to flee. It was a mistake I never made again.

There are many sophisticated travelers who "wing it" without reservations but it's unlikely they would attempt it during the busiest seasons. When I'm traveling with a friend I'm happy with a come-what-may approach, but on my own in a foreign country I enjoy the insurance of reservations and prefer to travel off-season when the natives are less frazzled and there is greater hope of connecting with them.

My approach puts me in the sissy category compared to Bess, who at age seventy-two rented out her house for seven months and with the bare bones of an itinerary set off with only her backpack to trek around the world.

"I'm afraid I'm not a very meticulous planner," she laughed. "I just get off the plane and ask someone to direct me to a hotel or hostel. In all the places I've visited, only once, in Africa, was I stuck for a place to sleep. Luckily, I met a man on the plane who opened his home to me. But that's all part of the adventure. I like to be surprised."

I stammered that this was more surprise than I was up for.

"When you backpacked through Cambodia, Africa and Tibet did you hike alone?" I asked.

"Well, for the most part, yes. Of course I always checked the U.S. travel advisory to make sure that I didn't get into anyone's line of fire. I'm not rash! But once I knew I was physically safe I felt quite happy on my own. I say 'on my own' but actually I met people everywhere; I was never by myself for long. On all the trips I've taken I've never felt at all lonely. Not once. The world is really full of kindly people happy to help you if need be. You don't always read about them in the papers but traveling has shown me they exist. Of course, you never know what might happen and you can't kid yourself. You learn about your fears (in my case of the heights I encountered while hiking to the base camp of Mount Everest) and you learn about your capabilities. After all, it's the challenge that makes us grow. The joy is in the struggle."

Although she may have endured more struggle than I care to embrace, Bess is my heroine. She shines at the extreme end of self-reliance.

At the other admirable extreme is Diane, who lives alone and has traveled throughout the world, in fact to many places Bess has visited. She, too, has never had a bad experience but her style differs radically. Her trips are meticulously planned. Every detail is carefully researched and plotted and she often goes with friends or depends on tour groups.

Everyone I interviewed, whether their touring style was improvised or controlled, spoke of traveling alone with exhilaration. Lori, who is in her thirties, became fascinated with Egyptology several years ago and has made many trips alone to Egypt. On one trip she heard about an oasis that sounded fascinating but that could only be reached by a ten-hour drive into the desert. She found a driver and rolled off in a Jeep across what appeared to be uncharted sand.

"Did you know where you'd spend the night?" I asked.

"No, but I was told in Cairo that there is a man who takes groups out in the desert to sleep!"

She spoke of the joy of being unhooked from her everyday world, free to follow her avid interests wherever they might lead and to toss out her itinerary if she heard of some local site she hadn't known about. Traveling with a companion might have dampened her own sense of adventure. She told me that not only has she never felt lonely but that, because her experiences with

people have been so reassuring, she actually feels pro-
tected when traveling alone in a foreign country.

❧

When it comes down to it, it's impossible to travel alone.
We're among people every step of the way unless we
decide to sail the Atlantic single-handedly. There's usually someone nearby with whom to share any marvel and
today with cell phones and computers it's hard to make a
case for ever being isolated and without resources. *We're
a human family; no matter what the language we can connect with others if we are open, curious and enthusiastic.*

WE ARE RARELY ALONE WHEN TRAVELING
BY OURSELVES IF WE'RE WILLING TO ACKNOWLEDGE
OTHERS ALONG THE WAY.

• *Identify the traveling style best suited to your temperament and needs.* If you're traveling alone for the first time you might consider a cruise or tour group. You'll be guaranteed a social life and have immediate access to experienced troubleshooters.

If you're going by yourself and prone to anxiety when away from home base, it's best to make hotel reservations ahead of time. If you'd prefer taking your chances and improvising on the outcome, it's easier if you travel off-season when there are more options for accommodations. Many people who travel alone take buses and trains in order to be free to enjoy the scenery while being among other travelers.

• *Consider traveling off-season.* The smaller the crowds the easier it is to book hotels and restaurants, and to find opportunities to converse with others. The museums and local sites are less mobbed, which allows for a more focused experience. Local residents and those working in hotels, restaurants, shops and museums are more relaxed and communicative and the possibility of getting to know other travelers is much more likely.

• *Research your destinations.* Get insider tips about restaurants, hotels and interesting places to visit from travel agents, books, the Internet and people who have been there. Knowing about the place beforehand gives you an advantage during your first days. Thereafter, seek information from the local tourist office, your hotel or people you meet along the way; there are often sites known only locally that could become the highlight of your trip. Be flexible and willing to jettison your itinerary in order to follow these suggestions.

• *Always call the U.S. travel advisory at 202-647-5225 (or check their Web site, www.travel.state.gov) before venturing into a troubled country.* Airlines can also provide information. In case of an emergency, it's helpful to have a list of contacts such as the American Embassy, the American Express office or, if possible, local residents referred by friends. Plan these backup contacts in advance; it's harder to figure things out if you're sick or in difficulty.

• *Practice eating in restaurants by yourself.* You'll usually find that there are others eating on their own as well. Enjoy the contact with them, those who wait on you, the atmosphere, other patrons. Even if there is little or no conversation between you and anyone there, don't consider yourself alone. You are not an isolated individual who has nothing in common with other people; everyone is sharing the experience of eating there. Be open to casual conversation when it feels comfortable.

• *Travel from an enthusiastic desire to see and experience new things, not as an attempt to escape loneliness or depression.* We tend to take our moods with us, and though a change of scene and being among others can be a balm to those feelings, there is no guarantee that we won't feel even more isolated. If things don't go as we hoped, the negative feelings are in place to help us exaggerate the difficulties. If you really need to get away, a good solution would be to go on a cruise or sign onto a tour. There you'll find activities and a social life that can lift your spirits.

• *Leave at home the agenda of meeting a romantic interest.* That way you lessen the risk of feeling disappointed if he or she doesn't materialize. Think of your trip as a personal adventure, an opportunity to explore your freedom and to just be yourself. If you happen to find someone who attracts you, that's fine, but a more realistic goal is simply to meet interesting people.

An artist produces for the liberation of his soul.
If he is successful, in the end, he will draw
a complete picture of himself.
—SOMERSET MAUGHAM

reaching in

(lovers may leave us, husbands and wives
may die, friends can move away, but
creativity remains faithfully ours)

"You're not yourself today" we're told as children when
we're out of sorts or moody. We're encouraged to be
our "real" self—the nice, sunny, reasonable one—and to
round up those maverick "selves," with their melancholies, griefs and angers, handcuff them and exile them
to the darker side of our psyches. There they languish
out of view (even our own view) conveniently forgotten

though we sometimes feel curiously incomplete. Living alone gives us the time and solitude to liberate those exiled selves and invite them into the light.

If it's important, as Rilke said, to "be pushed down into our hearts, otherwise we won't go there," surely the quickest route is *creativity, the crown jewel of solitude.*

Of course, anyone can be creative, but those of us who live alone are gifted with abundant time to ourselves, time to establish a personal arts colony, a dreaming space, a playing space. Here we're free to wander through our inner wilderness with its alluring melancholies and X-rated emotions, then return to the real world owning more of ourselves than when we first embarked.

The paths are many; writing is one. Whether we confess our thoughts to a journal, explore them in fiction or launch into the orbit of poetry, writing can lead us "down into our hearts" where our multitudinous selves are clamoring to be reclaimed.

One evening I was sharing dinner with my friend Bartolo and I playfully suggested that we write a poem

together. He looked alarmed and waved off my pro-
posal.

"I'm not a poet," he laughed. "I've read very little
poetry and don't have a poet's vocabulary or images. Or
content, for that matter. No! Not for me!"

"But you're a singer and appreciate beautiful lyrics,"
I objected.

"Singing a lyric," he insisted, "is far different than
composing one." He ordered a brandy.

I jotted down a line and pushed the notebook to his
side of the table. He read what I'd written, then sighed
and scribbled something to indulge me. He then passed
me the notebook and took a gulp of brandy. After a
number of "turns" the poem seemed to be finished and I
read it to him. He was pleasantly taken aback.

"It must be the brandy," he said self-consciously and
asked for the check.

The following day he phoned. "May I read you
something?"

He then read a long poem filled with images of
childhood—of love and loss—written in the kind of language that he never would use in everyday life.

"You've written a beautiful poem," I said. "I'm so
touched by it."

"I didn't write it."

"Really? Who did?"

"I don't know," he puzzled. "Some guy wrote it through me. Some stranger. I don't know who he is, but he certainly isn't me. I can't write like that!"

During the next year Bartolo wrote more than one hundred poems about the world of this stranger. He found him in the half-light of memory on the furious frontiers of his childhood. He had begun resurrecting his exiled selves.

Because Bartolo lives alone he was always on call to catch the unexpected offerings tossed up from his unconscious. When this "stranger" within him needed to speak Bartolo didn't have to postpone their communion or retreat behind a door to find the solitude so dear to the act of creation. At midnight or dawn, in the middle of a meal or driving in his car, Bartolo wrote and wrote undisturbed by obligations to a partner. *When we live alone time and freedom are at the service of our muse in a way that artists in a relationship might envy.*

When my love for reading led me to writing I was at first defeated by inhibition. The poet Wallace Stevens spoke of going up to his office in the attic after dinner and "stepping across the line." But many of us cower at the edge of that psychological boundary and abort our soul's adventure.

I turned to my friend Jan Stussy, the most prolific painter I knew.

"How did you develop the courage?" I asked.

"When I was in the tenth grade," he said, "I realized that if you simply make the first mark, the rest will just happen. Whether it's that first mark with a brush on a canvas or pencil to paper, boldly make it and then let yourself free-fall. Art creates art."

"Free-fall?" It sounded perilous.

"Like jumping off a high-dive. Walk out there. Don't think. Don't look down. Just dive!"

I tried it. I sat down with paper and pen and just wrote, recklessly, without judgment, without spell-check. It was like going deliciously mad on the page! Where did these feelings come from? Who was feeling them? Who was writing such odd thoughts and images? Each time I surfaced I came back with a strange creature I treasured. Whether the world would equally treasure my captives wasn't important; they were mine and I welcomed them home like family.

꩜

After some time passed, I would revisit my wild creatures and try to understand what they were attempting to say. Often I'd smooth their frayed edges and make them presentable. But my favorite ones didn't want to be civilized; they were revealing secrets for my eyes only. I put them in a special notebook called the "Storm Pages." In the privacy of these leaves, no thought was censored, no longing unexpressed, no anger unclaimed. It was a shelter for the selves in the back of the cage, those that snarl and grieve, those that frolic in dream and recoil in nightmare.

The Storm Pages became my route to self-revelation. In them I experienced events of the day in slow motion, more powerfully in retrospect than I could as they whizzed by in real time. I dared to be truthful, to record not what I wished I had felt but what I, in truth, actually did feel. Writing had become a way of honoring my authentic selves.

The most fertile time for me to dive into my unconscious was soon after I woke up. In silence and undisturbed privacy I would sit in my bathrobe and write until I was sated. When I'd been in a relationship I dreamed of writing and occasionally did but I didn't have the *continuity of solitude to sustain it.* Usually by the time we finished breakfast and shared the newspaper, the activities of the day flooded in and crowded out the fragile voices of my dream world. At night I enjoyed social activities and finally exhaustion blew out my muse's candle.

❧

Mine is a shy muse that approaches slowly—only in silence—and flutters away at the slightest disturbance. We are like the Fox and the Little Prince in Saint-Exupery's story: When the Little Prince asks the Fox how they can become friends he says if they sit in silence at opposite ends of a field every day, after a long time they will be friends. We are both the Little Prince and the Fox and need a long time in our solitary field to become close to ourselves. A writer once commented that after he was left alone for long periods of time he felt larger than before. That *alone time is the elixir of the artist; singles are blessed with it.* I wrote more in the first year I was living on my own than I had in my entire life.

❧

We create in order to become whole. We may choose to share our creations with the world. Or we may not. When friends found out about the Storm Pages, they asked if I intended to publish them. I didn't; it would have been like trying to publish my prayers. The internal rewards are great whether we share our efforts or not; *where our most fervent selves are engaged at the peak of our capacity there is rapture.*

It's unrealistic to expect to be completely accepted and understood in life. If we're lucky there will be a friend or two who will encourage the grand avalanche of our inner lives. Or maybe a good therapist. But our art will never let us down. It is there to contain as much as we are willing to express.

Rilke, the superstar of solitude, said, "and in those silent times when something mysterious is drawing near I want to be with those who know secret things or else alone." I suspect that the "something mysterious drawing near" is our abandoned selves. We are each an archive of our own "secret things" approaching with their unwept tears and hidden dreams.

I like to imagine a trunk brought up from the deep

in which all the evidence of our selves has been gathered, a personal treasure like the Storm Pages harboring furies that we're too civilized to expose or extravagant love effusions that would sink any suitor. In it is packed evidence of our inner truth that proves we are larger selves than the world has encouraged us to accept.

Lovers may leave us, husbands and wives may die, friends can move away, but creativity is faithfully ours if we honor our solitude by diving to realms that are deeper, freer and more complete than our surface lives. Once we know the way we can come home to it anytime we wish—if we *make the first mark*.

Don't think. Don't look down. Just dive!

CREATIVITY IS THE QUICKEST ROUTE
TO OUR TRUEST SELVES.

• *List the artistic interests you've been drawn to but have hesitated to pursue.* If you're a reader perhaps you've wanted to write; if music has interested you it may be singing or songwriting, or perhaps you remember the pleasure of painting in art class in school. You can get inspiration from reading, looking at art or listening to your favorite songs. But the point is to use these art forms to express without reservation your truest feelings. Don't limit yourself to one pursuit if others also attract you. If you're verbal and inclined to write, consider a secondary avenue of expression like painting or music.

• *Determine the best time to get in touch with the deeper part of yourself and try to consistently make it available.* Some prefer to work when they first get up, others late at night when there are no distractions. Organize your week in such a way that will ensure you will find the time to paint, write, sing or compose. Consistency will bring about the deepest rewards.

• *Collect the tools of creativity: notebooks, paints, brushes, musical instruments.* Keep them in a special place where they are readily available. Some people prefer to work in the same spot each day as if the muse is accustomed to finding them there.

• *Make the first mark. Walk out there. Don't think. Don't look down. Just dive!* Be reckless. What's the worst that can happen? We're hoping to be surprised by some unrestrained part of ourselves that can't be expressed in our ordinary lives. The discoveries we're after can only surprise us when we're ready to accept whatever we uncover. If journal writing interests you make a special Storm Pages version that is for your eyes alone. In it express your most excessive feelings in detailed and descriptive language. It's our birthright to claim all of our selves, not just the most socially acceptable ones. Relish the freedom.

• *Don't judge your creation. Accept it with gratitude.* What we express is a valuable part of ourselves and worthy of our respect. If you want to send it out into the world to compete with other artists, then study and work toward that goal. But, even then, there should be a safe, noncompetitive shelter for our wildest productions;

they are the ones that reveal and unleash our shackled selves.

• *Develop the habit of reaching in. It's a way to come home to ourselves, to be whole.* Those who consistently express themselves feel homesick if, from time to time, they are unable to. If you're on a trip take along a notebook or small set of watercolors. There is no reason we should leave all our selves behind—we are always good company!

At every place and time throughout your life,
take frankly what that place and time
can give you, and think of its limitation
as advantage rather than harm.
—JOHN RUSKIN

coda

Rilke wrote, "I want to unfold. I do not want to stay folded anywhere, for where I am folded, there I am a lie." No matter how perilous it may seem at first—with its imagined isolation and vulnerabilities—living alone invites us to unfold as fully as possible.

A few years ago I held a Christmas gathering. Worried that a guest might bring me an unexpected present that I would want to reciprocate, I bought a number of amaryllis bulbs packaged in cardboard boxes with complicated interfolding tops and parked them in the back of my bedroom closet, just in case. During the party I gave most of them away. Three months later, as I was walking through my bedroom, something caught my eye. Reaching out from under the bottom of my closet door was a pale green tongue. Puzzled, I followed this strange object back through the closet to a forgotten amaryllis box. The frond had fought its way through the complicated folds of the lid and onto the floor to partake of the light under the door. When I carried the box into the room and opened it my knees nearly buckled. In its effort to fulfill its amaryllis destiny the bulb had unfurled in its dark prison; its stem was knotted around itself, its crimson blossoms lay partially opened and decaying.

The amaryllis, trying to unfold in its specially constructed box, is a metaphor for many of us who, from ignorance or fear, have locked away our potential in the back of our mental closets constructed from society's attitudes about how things "should be." To flower we must seek the sunlight of possibilities, dare to own ourselves and lead lives that are valuable simply because we are leading them fully. There is a beautiful quote from the recently discovered buried Gospel according to Thomas attributed to Christ: "If you bring forth what is within you, what you bring forth will save you. If you do not bring forth what is within you, what you do not bring forth will destroy you."

Living alone makes us entrepreneurs of our destiny. Once we've established our individual interests and closeness to others, the silent spaces between events no longer feel empty. We can even enjoy the anarchy of doing nothing, just staring out the window, puttering about, playfully luxuriating in time the way an otter does in water. In other words, as Gerard Manley Hopkins wrote, "What I do is me. For this I came."

❧

The writer Dory Previn tells a story about driving around at night when she lived in California, and each time she saw a light in the window of a house she would think, "That person has found the secret to happiness." One night, momentarily lost, she turned down a road, saw a light in a window and again thought, "That person has found the secret of happiness." Then she realized it was her own house!

Being on one's own isn't always ideal, but then, neither is marriage or anything else in life. Alone we simply shift our spotlight from a partner to focusing more inclusively on the world and oneself. We can reach out and we can also reach in.

I've interviewed many singles who have spoken in praise of living alone. Those who grew up with closeness and affection find it easy and natural. Those who were lonely as children had to learn that, as adults, they have a world of people and options at their disposal. But they all share three basic characteristics: curiosity, enthusiasm and the wish to celebrate life by living fully. Edna St. Vincent Millay captured it beautifully when she wrote, *"Oh, world, I cannot hold thee close enough!"*

about the author

Barbara Feldon is best known for her role as Secret Agent "99" on the hit TV series *Get Smart*. A feminist and activist, she lectures on behalf of women and girls. Feldon has served on the board of the Screen Actors Guild, the Poetry Society of America and the Orchestra of St. Luke's. She lives in New York City.